DIALOGIC READERS

Dialogic Readers: Children talking and thinking together about visual texts celebrates the sophisticated and dynamic discussions that primary-aged children can have as they talk together to make meaning from a variety of texts, and it highlights the potential for talk between readers as a tool for critical and creative thinking. It proposes a new dialogic theory of reading comprehension that incorporates multi-modal media and adds further weight to the argument that talk as a tool for learning should form a central part of primary classroom learning and teaching.

The book explores:

- the language of co-construction
- children's critical and creative response to text
- the dialogic transaction between text and readers
- the use of language as a tool for creating a social cohesion between readers

This significant work is aimed at educational lecturers, researchers and students who want to explore an expanded notion of reading comprehension in the twenty-first century, realizing how opportunities for children thinking creatively together might transform the potential for learning in the classroom. It provides a framework for analyzing co-constructive talk with suggestions for promoting children's critical and creative thinking.

Fiona Maine is a lecturer in literacy education at the University of Cambridge with many years of experience working with teachers as they develop their own practice. Prior to her teacher educator roles, she worked as a primary classroom teacher.

DIALOGIC READERS

Children talking and thinking together about visual texts

Fiona Maine

Routledge
Taylor & Francis Group

LONDON AND NEW YORK

First published 2015
by Routledge
2 Park Square, Milton Park, Abingdon, Oxon OX14 4RN

and by Routledge
711 Third Avenue, New York, NY 10017

Routledge is an imprint of the Taylor & Francis Group, an informa business

© 2015 Fiona Maine

British Library Cataloguing-in-Publication Data
A catalogue record for this book is available from the British Library

Library of Congress Cataloging in Publication Data
A catalog record for this book has been requested

ISBN: 978-0-415-72807-2 (hbk)
ISBN: 978-0-415-72808-9 (pbk)
ISBN: 978-1-315-71821-7 (ebk)

Typeset in Bembo
by Swales & Willis Ltd, Exeter, Devon, UK

CONTENTS

ILLUSTRATIONS

Figures

Tables

ACKNOWLEDGEMENTS

Thanks must first go to the wonderful children in this study whose creativity and enthusiasm reminded me every day that we should stop and listen carefully to what children say. Thanks also to their wonderful teachers who were flexible, helpful and happy to try out some new ideas. Thanks to Shiel Taylor for so warmly welcoming me into her school to work with the children there and for being a career-long supportive friend.

Academic advice, support and encouragement came from Chris White, Stephen Ward, Dan Davies, Rupert Wegerif, Robert Fisher, Teresa Cremin, Frank Hardman and Tim Middleton. Colleagues and friends to thank for their involvement and support are Viki Bennett, Nicki Henderson, Emma Asprey, Joelle Adams, Charles Sisum, Robin Shields, Nick Sorensen, Ruth Barrington, Steve Coombs, Penny Summers and Kevin Eames. For some early inspiration, I am grateful to Alan Howe, Steve Bicknell and the late great Pat D'Arcy.

Particular thanks to Alison Waller and Elaine Lam for helping me realize that the mountain could be climbed, and to Professor Christine Eden for continued support, challenge, and mentoring.

1

INTRODUCTION

An answer is always the stretch of road that's behind you. Only a question can point the way forward.

(Gaarder, 1997: 31)

Louis, Josh and *Baboon on the Moon*

Louis and Josh, both aged six, have watched *Baboon on the Moon* (Duriez, 2003). In the film, a baboon is seen living in a house on the moon, going about his everyday business. He gets up, has breakfast, then goes to a shed, where he tips 'moonshine' into a machine which then lights up the moon. The final part of the film shows the baboon sitting down, removing a trumpet from a case and playing it while looking at a far-off Earth. A tear runs down his cheek. The two children have been asked to talk about what the film is 'all about' and ask questions about it, and moments of this exchange have been captured on video. The transcript of these exchanges is as follows:

Josh	How did he get on the moon?
Louis	I think he might of, on Earth and he got this control which was for his house, then he pressed a wrong button, then his house turned into a space rocket. Then he pressed another button and it went up to the moon.
Josh	Maybe he . . .
Louis	. . . heard, you know in the film, did you hear a space rocket sound in it?
Josh	(nods)
Louis	So I might be right.

Josh   Yeah we are right! . . . I can't believe we found that out! How does the postman get there every day?

Louis   What, to Baboon's house?

Josh   Yeah.

Louis   I don't know.

Josh   But how can the postman deliver the post?

Louis   Yeah . . . Oh he might have a letter . . . to shoot the letters up to Earth! Up to it, the moon. Shoot the letters up! In a big bag!

Josh   But how can the postman get the letters and put it in his house, on the moon? Maybe he has to get a rocket and some choppers and things.

Louis   Yeah, that's what he has!

The children are reading the film, making sense of its moving image through co-constructing a narrative that is plausible to them both. They are able to read the film through constructing a story that not only interprets what they see on the screen but also moves beyond the frame of this visual text to give an explanation for what is presented. They are not bound by the images on screen, but use these as a springboard for meaning-making, drawing on their existing knowledge of the world and particular interests (choppers! rockets!) to understand what they see. Importantly, with this wordless visual narrative, their meaning-making is not hindered by their ability (or otherwise) to decode written text, and their cognitive capacities can be directed entirely to the process of comprehension, rather than the labour of unlocking the alphabetic code first.

The exchanges between Louis and Josh take moments and represent a snapshot of the wider discussions that were happening within the classroom. Yet they can be analyzed from multiple theoretical perspectives, providing layer upon layer of insight into the different processes involved, and building a rich picture of the children's discussion. There are different reflections that can start to uncover the dynamics of this exchange. These include analyzing how the children's language supports their collaborative meaning-making and what the thinking processes that underpin this language might be. In addition, as this is a joint task, the approach that the children take to socially negotiating the task can be considered. Certain linguistic features in the children's discussion can be seen as indicators of collaborative meaning-making. For example, in the following extract, the children ask 'how' questions and suggest ideas using 'might' and 'maybe'. These incidences could be counted to analyze the frequency with which these words are used by the children in fulfilling the task at hand:

Louis   Yeah . . . Oh he <u>might</u> have a letter . . . to shoot the letters up to Earth! Up to it, the moon. Shoot the letters up! In a big bag!

Josh   But <u>how</u> can the postman get the letters and put it in his house, on the moon? <u>Maybe</u> he has to get a rocket and some choppers and things.

The suggestion of ideas, using language such as 'maybe' and 'might', could also be seen to highlight the social interaction apparent in the discourse. The children propose ideas to each other so that solutions can be found collaboratively. Additionally, an advantage of asking them to engage in the task together allows access to their thinking, indicated through the language they use, which gives some insight into the specific critical thinking skills they appear to use to comprehend the picture:

Josh How did he get on the moon?
Louis I think he might of, on Earth and he got this control which was for his house, then he pressed a wrong button, then his house turned into a space rocket. Then he pressed another button and it went up to the moon.

In the extract above, Josh decides on a problem to be solved; that is, how the baboon came to be on the moon. Then Louis tries to find a solution, using the skill of rationalizing possibilities that help him to make sense of the problem. The critical skill of problem-solving is extended by Louis' creative thinking when he makes a suggestion that exists outside the existing world of the film. There is no evidence to suggest that the house is, in fact, a space rocket that has landed on the moon, so he must have created the idea based on his own experience or mental model of the world (Wells, 2009). His interpretation possibly demonstrates specific cultural influences that enable him to link *rockets* and the *moon*. To comprehend meaning, the children raise questions and then predict possible answers, drawing on their existing knowledge of stories and films. The children, at six years old, already have a wealth of cultural experience that can lead them to quickly classify information into difference categories of understanding, to assimilate the information into their existing schema. The knowledge they have is dependent on the cultural context in which they have lived so far (Rogoff, 2003), as had they been born into a different cultural context, they may not have experienced the same phenomena to lead to this connection.

Taking a more philosophical approach that is less concerned with cognitive processes and more focused on the quality of the talk allows us to consider if the children are engaged in 'good thinking' (Moseley et al., 2005: 19), their awareness of their thinking process, and how they are engaging in the task. Josh says, 'Yeah we are right! . . . I can't believe we found that out!' in response to Louis' suggestion that there might be a rocket. He shows pleasure at Louis' suggestion, deciding that the problem has been solved, but his language can also be seen to imply that this was a meaning hidden in the text, suggesting he feels that they have been engaged in 'good thinking' to have worked this out. The comment also suggests an awareness of the context of the conversation. The children have a task to complete, assigned to them by a teacher, and Josh is commenting on the successful undertaking of that task by showing that he is able to monitor his own thinking and make judgements about it.

The short samples above demonstrate that these different viewpoints can bring additional depth to the analysis that is possible from one short communication, and they help us unravel what is happening when children co-construct meaning. It is from this position that the enquiry in this book began. The question was whether taking a multi-layered analytical approach could offer a broader and more holistic view of children's meaning-making processes, particularly in relation to visual texts. Would this approach illuminate what the actual process of co-constructing meaning from text can be extended to include? Exploring thinking and language together opens up the consideration of the inter-mental (Vygotsky, 1978; Mercer and Littleton, 2007) processes in action, or talk as a 'social mode of thinking' (Mercer, 1995: 4), and combining theories about language and comprehension leads to a dialogic perspective on reading. Setting models of comprehension against models of thinking places the importance of critical and creative thinking at the centre of making meaning from text.

This book introduces the idea of a dialogic perspective on reading, which will be explored fully in later chapters. However, a brief consideration of the notion of the *dialogic* is appropriate here. The term stems from the original work of Bakhtin (1981), and describes the nature of the linguistic exchanges that happen within a discussion. The essence of *dialogue* and *dialogic* (as pertaining to *dialogue*) is that of 'implied response' and it can be argued that 'all language is dialogic' (Lyle, 2008: 224) if there is always the possibility of response from a listener to an utterance by a speaker. Dialogue then, is concerned with communication, and in particular, the transaction of meaning between speakers. There is a wealth of research that concentrates on classroom dialogue (for example, Sinclair and Coulthard, 1975; Nystrand et al., 1997), and more recently this focus on the importance of language for learning has been embraced within models of dialogic teaching (Alexander, 2003, 2008). This book is a study of children's talk, yet it does not focus on teacher dialogue, only talk between peers, or pupil–pupil dialogue. However, it does centralize the importance of talk as 'an object of learning in its own right' (Alexander, 2003: 6) by focusing on the dialogue of pairs of children reading visual texts together. In addition, the principles underpinning a dialogic classroom (Alexander, 2008) are a prerequisite to this type of pupil engagement as they mean that the children are confident and competent in sharing their views, and are able to do so without the direct input of the teacher.

While other sociocultural studies (for example Lyle, 1993; Barnes and Todd, 1995; Mercer, 1995, 1996, 2000, 2004; Mercer et al., 1999; Mercer and Littleton, 2007; Littleton and Mercer, 2013) have explored different modes of talk, this study develops an analytical framework that illuminates the dialogic and co-constructive functions of the language the children use as they make meaning from visual texts together. Reznitskaya et al. (2009) highlight the importance of empirical research that develops and applies analytical frameworks of this kind, as they argue that it provides an opportunity to move beyond idealized notions of dialogue. While the research can be broadly located within the field of 'sociocultural discourse analysis' (Mercer, 2004), the different approach it offers is the specific consideration of the dialogic processes that are evidenced in co-constructive talk when children inquire together to make sense of visual texts. If to inquire is to question, and to ask questions leads to an active engagement with the world (Donaldson, 1978), then this is an important activity. Educationalists as far back as Dewey (1933) have emphasized the importance of teaching children to think and inquire. This research assumes that children should be encouraged to embrace the purpose of inquiry – to find meaning and make sense of the world with 'ardent curiosity, fertile imagination and love of experimental inquiry' (Dewey, 1933: v) –and that this is a prerequisite to meaningful educational approaches.

Applying this to literacy and in particular reading is important as it enables the process of reading comprehension to become visible. Using reading as a stimulus for discussion allows an exploration of the critical and creative thinking processes involved in meaning-making, which is viewed as a dialogic process between readers together and between text and readers (Maine, 2013). The children are working together to solve the problem of what the texts might mean, and they are doing this within the context of the classroom (see Figure 1.1).

The book is an exploration of primary-aged children's dialogic responses to visual text. The texts that the children encountered in the study varied in mode (pictures, moving image media, picturebooks) but all had a visual element in common. Seeing texts as signifiers of meaning (Barthes, 1977, 1981; Kress, 2003) means that the notion of reading is not constrained to the decoding of the written word, but includes visual and multi-modal forms. Indeed, texts with a written element were not used for children who would find decoding words difficult. Many of the texts used offered multiple reading pathways (as defined by Barthes, 1977, 1981; Kress and van Leeuwen, 1996; Kress, 2003) and while an entire debate could centre on the affordances of specific images to provoke different types of discussion, the

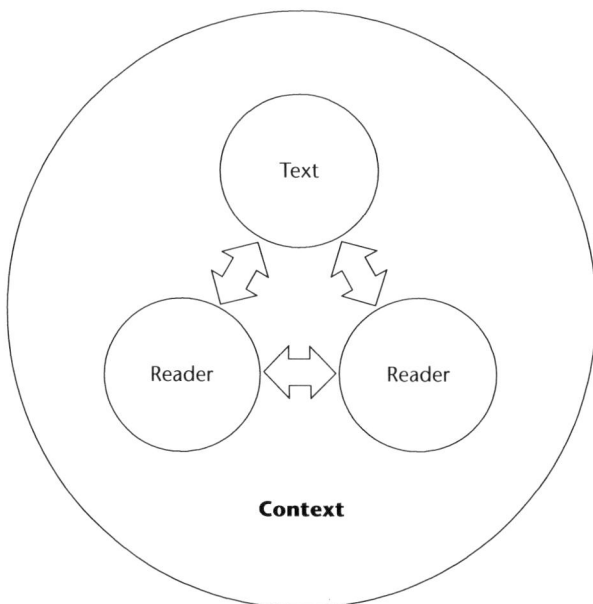

FIGURE 1.1 A model of dialogic reading

leading principle behind the selection of any particular text was that it served as a provocation or springboard for children to think together through talk, and engage together as dialogic readers.

Overview of chapters

To give a sense of the whole book, an overview of each chapter is included here. The chapters build on each other to form a theoretical framework for dialogic reading, leading to a consideration of how these ideas might be implemented in the primary classroom.

Chapter 2 is the core chapter and sets the theoretical underpinnings of the book. Key ideas are explored here, starting by broadly locating the research within the tradition of sociocultural study. This is the wide-angled lens, considering the way that children learn and highlighting the importance of talk and dialogue in this process. The chapter then focuses more closely on what this means for understandings about reading comprehension, by clearly defining 'text' and 'reading' to include multi-modal forms (including visual and moving image) and arguing that this is essential in 21st-century notions of literacy. At this point the chapter brings together theories of dialogue with sociocultural theories of reading to propose a dialogic understanding of reading as a transaction between text and respondent(s). Finally, the chapter introduces the research data, briefly outlining the study and its context.

Chapter 3 looks in detail at the language these dialogic readers use as they co-construct meaning from text. It focuses on the role of speech moves (called co-constructive moves) in generating and maintaining discussion and how while these might be typified by particular language indicators, their importance lies in their function rather than the exact words used. Ten different co-constructive moves are coded in vignettes of children talking together, and the moves are compared across the data. Taking the vignettes as whole discussions, the concept of a *dialogic space of possibility* between speakers is proposed and the affordance of different response moves to open or close the conversation is explored. Moves that open the dialogue and offer possibilities for discussion are regarded as divergent moves, and those that close the dialogue by offering little affordance for continued co-construction are regarded as convergent moves. The chapter leads to a theoretical model of co-constructive dialogue and the concept of dialogic chains of thinking that link different turns together.

In Chapter 4 the thinking indicated in the vignettes is explored in more detail, and the notion of divergent (creative) and convergent (critical) moves is used as a springboard to discuss creative and critical thinking as apparent in the children's talk. The chapter starts by considering the differences between critical and creative thinking and how these ultimately work together in problem-solving. It moves on to explore the language that seems to indicate different modes of thinking in the children's talk and how ideas are developed and linked through chains in their dialogue. The task of making meaning from the text together is presented as a problem-solving activity, so the chapter explores the children's pursuit of resolution in their discussion and how they settle on ideas or return to previous ones.

Chapter 5 looks at the transaction of meaning-making between the text and the readers, remembering that many of the texts are purely visual rather than having a written element. It highlights the different strategies the dialogic readers use to engage with and make sense of the texts. Linking back to the ideas espoused in the preceding chapter, the comprehension strategies the children use are regarded as critical and creative problem-solving skills. This time, the notion of dialogic space is set between text and reader. The data are examined to demonstrate how the readers respond by determining the importance of different features or key moments in the text; making connections to their existing schema; and asking questions and making predictions to hypothesize. The dialogic readers widen and deepen this metaphorical space first by extending the world of the text to create narratives to explain it, and second by entering the text-world and empathizing with characters within it, or placing themselves in the 'scene'. The approach the readers take is common to both written and visual texts. These 'entanglement' (Iser, 1978) strategies are important as they allow the children to create meanings from a different standpoint. They also allow a 'negative capability' (Keats et al., 2002) or poetic creativity where the enjoyment of exploring the ideas that are generated does not need resolution or neat conclusion. This is the essence of creative meaning-making, and enables children to think beyond the box, delighting in their own creativity.

In Chapter 6, attention turns to the *process* of meaning-making: children's awareness of the task and their ability to reflect on it. Metacognition and reflection are identified as crucial parts of both critical and creative thinking, and key comprehension strategies as readers check that the meaning they have made is plausible. The children also demonstrate an awareness of their own thinking; they regulate their management of the task of reading and draw on shared cultural understandings to co-construct meaning, reminding us that these literacy events occur in a specific sociocultural context.

Also focusing on the process of the task at hand, in Chapter 7 attention is turned to the children's management of the discussion as a social enterprise. The chapter considers how the use of ambiguous, hypothetical language supports the social harmony between the children and allows them to negotiate ideas, sometimes appearing to agree with each other when in fact they are disagreeing. The language of this social cohesion is explored in depth, in particular through the use of connective words and phrases and creativity in language play. The chapter proposes that what is elsewhere defined as cumulative talk (for example, Mercer, 2000, 2004), and sometimes overlooked as it appears to be low-level thinking, can actually serve as a social prerequisite to discussion, and that maintaining a social harmony is the foundation of more exploratory talk. Moreover, children use language to establish inter-subjectivity between themselves, through pausing, repeating words and following language patterns. They are playful in their language use and their humour takes a role in establishing a solid social foundation for their creative thinking.

The final chapter of the book brings the ideas together by considering the implications of the theory for educational practice. It is titled 'From research into practice' to remind the reader that educational research has a responsibility to the development of improved practice, and that by engaging with theoretical thinking, policy makers and practitioners are better able to understand children's development and therefore plan curriculum and pedagogy accordingly. The chapter proposes a broad analytical framework for co-constructive talk, with suggestions for promoting the language that children use in their creative response to text. Finally, the chapter returns to the idea of a dialogic theory of reading comprehension in which talk and creative thinking are paramount as a theory fit for the purposes of 21st-century literacy.

2

MAKING MEANING TOGETHER AND FROM TEXT

Making meaning together

We engage with the world by asking questions of it. We are active, interactive learners who seek to understand our reality by making connections to what we already know and exploring the possibilities of what we do not know. Our own realities are shaped by the experiences we have, the values that have been taught to us and individually formed and the sense we have made of these. Central to this understanding of the world is our ability to communicate, to listen to and talk with others, to hear their stories and, through gaining insight into their perception, crystallize our own thinking. We represent the world to each other and move together to make a collective sense of it. Our world therefore is socially constructed, with individuals interpreting any situation from their own standpoint and communicating this with others. As each moment of interpretation is located in space and time, historical and cultural influences affect all perspectives. Therefore, our existing understanding of the way the world works is continually constructed and reconstructed. Experiences are used to inform judgements about new situations, with the resulting world view extended by identifying patterns and connecting to these previous experiences.

Piaget's theories suggested new knowledge is *assimilated* into existing schemas or *accommodated* by creating new schemas (cited in Wood, 1998: 53). Our hypotheses about life lead to an interpretation of the world and reality, with new situations either fitting into an existing schema or causing an adjustment of thinking to 'accommodate' a new phenomenon. This, of course, does not just relate to children; the human experience means making sense of the world around us by drawing on previous experiences to judge how to act or respond, and this relates to all people, whatever their age. An interesting reflection is that as we grow older we become less inclined to 'accommodate', rather choosing to assimilate new experiences with previous ones. How many times, on visiting a new destination or meeting new people, do we comment, 'this reminds me of . . . ', or 'do you remember the time when we . . . ?' We continually seek to link to the security of what is known. Children just have fewer experiences with which to link.

The important assumption here is that the world is not merely passively received, but actively participated in. As Donaldson argues, 'We do not just sit and wait for the world to impinge on us. We try actively to interpret it and to make sense of it. We grapple with it, we construe it intellectually, we *represent it to ourselves*' [Donaldson's emphasis] (1978: 68). Based on this, the naivety (in its truest, non-detrimental sense) of children could mean a refreshing interpretation of the world, one that is not bound by experience and the motivation to pigeonhole but a genuine exploration of ideas in which literally anything is possible. Each new experience can be interpreted differently, without the need to relate it to an existing structure. However, this can be difficult, as without any links at all, and if everything was inexplicable or unrelated to other experiences, the world would be a baffling place. Sense is made by making connections.

Piaget describes how children, in their desire to make meaning, 'fill in the gaps' (1959: 126) in their understandings, and accept their solutions as legitimate without questioning the meaning intended. They are, he argues, uncritical in their acceptance of order, and in fact construct meanings together that further support their logic. His term 'justification at all costs' (1959: 145) is a suggestion that children search for a reason in everything, that they do not conceive an element of chance, and that this is part of their meaning-making process. A balance is needed. On the one hand, the idea that there is not just one correct interpretation, or tidy solution, offers a multitude of possibilities; yet it could equally be a confounding and frustrating experience to continually experience the world with such divergent thinking. However, the desire to justify and reason without taking a critical stance and evaluating the meaning taken is equally limiting, and offers a convergent and narrow perspective of the world. The balance occurs through the experience of both: being open to opportunities and possible alternatives to one's existing views, while drawing on one's own experiences and knowledge to make connections and synthesize.

The role of narrative in meaning-making

Whether accommodating or assimilating new knowledge, a key factor in making meaning is the construction of narrative or stories. Searching for a plausible narrative solution can answer issues of motivation, purpose and outcome. Narrative is, as Hardy famously declares, 'a primary act of mind' (Hardy, 1977: 12). Experiences are made sense of through the stories created about them, an idea further developed by Wells who points out that stories offer an opportunity to share experience, to collectively make sense of the world. He argues that,

although storying may have its roots in the biologically given human pre-
disposition to construct mental stories in order to make sense of perceptual
information, it very quickly becomes the means whereby we enter into a
shared social world, which is continually broadened and enriched by the
exchange of stories with others.

(Wells, 2009: 216)

The emphasis is thus placed onto the experience of a 'shared world', one in which
children create and share their narratives as a joint venture, to involve each other in
their story-worlds. That an educational context should encourage their disposition
to do this is then not surprising, nor should it be seen as unusual. Lyle's research
concludes that narrative understanding can be viewed as '*the* major cognitive tool
through which all human beings in all cultures make sense of the world' [Lyle's
emphasis] (2000: 53). Of course, children are given opportunities to jointly define
and create stories about the world they experience both within and beyond the
educational setting of the school, but this book explores what is actually happening
linguistically, cognitively and socially when they engage in this activity within a
classroom context.

Bruner (1986) also picks up the thread of the significance of narrative when
he defines two modes of thinking: logico-scientific and narrative. He defines the
logico-scientific mode of thought as the one concerned with 'a formal mathe-
matical system of description and explanation' (1986: 12). Conversely, it is the
application of the narrative mode that 'leads instead to gripping drama, [and] believ-
able (though not necessarily "true") historical accounts' (1986: 13). However, the
division of these modes does not account for the ability to engage both modes of
thinking simultaneously, just as Piaget's claim for 'justification at all costs' does not
accommodate the ability both to imagine and to reason. The research described
in this book provided opportunities for children to use both modes of thinking
to make meaning: the problem-solving, logico-scientific mode (which could be
defined as the more convergent and critical mode, perhaps aimed at 'justification'),
and the story-spinning, imaginative, narrative mode (a creative, divergent mode
of thinking).

The creation of stories and sense-making narratives then necessarily involves
hypotheses as to the nature of what is experienced. In other words, sense of the
world is created by asking questions to construct stories about it, and this state of
questioning and hypothesizing is a natural instinct. This is a positive disposition of
hypothetical wondering and then testing because 'we are, by nature, questioners.
We approach the world by wondering about it, entertaining hypotheses which we
are eager to check' (Donaldson, 1978: 68).

The positive consequence of this questioning disposition is that it not only supports a sense of how things are, but also offers a world of possibility by the consideration of how things might be, of what the world could be like. To hypothesize,
one must feel disposed to find out, and so at the centre of an interaction with the
surrounding world lies curiosity, an innate desire to *find out*.

A sociocultural perspective on meaning-making

The development of understanding does not happen in de-contextualized isolation, as reality is socially constructed and humans are active participants in a culturally specific social world. The foundation of this thinking lies with the work of Vygotsky whose theories around inter-subjectivity and the social nature of learning (1962; 1978) have greatly influenced current perspectives on thought and language. By recognizing that meanings are constructed, inter-mentally (or 'inter-psychologically'), and intra-mentally (or 'intra-psychologically'), Vygotsky places social context at the heart of learning and development. In other words, joint meanings are created by communicating with each other, in addition to the meanings that are formed by an individual as they interpret the world. Taking this idea further, Bakhtin emphasizes the dialogic nature of that world, arguing that response is a key driver to meaning-making, and Wegerif (2008a) argues that it is the linking of the theories of Bakhtin and Vygotsky (essentially starting with the work of Wertsch in 1991) that form the foundation of a sociocultural perspective. Wertsch (1991: 4) argues that: 'We need to develop the type of theoretical frameworks that can be understood and extended by researchers from a range of what now exist as separate disciplinary perspectives.'

The research that forms a backdrop for this book uses an inclusive theoretical frame which embraces social semiotics as part of a family of inter-related sociocultural perspectives (as recognized by Gavelek and Bresnahan, 2009). Therefore, the language that occurs to enable the social co-construction of meanings is central to this perspective, as well as the recognition of the social context in which it occurs. As Harre argues, 'all human action should be thought of in terms of its contribution to the developing discourse' and the 'potent things in the human world are not the people but the things that they say, the component speech acts of the conversations that are the tesserae of the mosaic of human converse' (Harre, 1990: 351). In other words, while the processes employed in perceiving the world are important, a reality with meaning is constructed through discussion and description. Of course, as argued above, each individual brings different experiences to bear, meaning there is any number of different possible interpretations of the world and these are dependent on a cultural situation. Furthermore, if this is so then 'children acquire the socially constructed psychological concepts, language and patterns of action which are available to them within their culture' (Pollard, 1996: 5). A sociocultural perspective therefore rejects the notion of 'universals' (Wertsch, 1991: 18), as each individual operates within the context that they find themselves. Moreover, their shared cultural discourse offers particular experiences to be encountered and this means that children's development can only be understood in the light of these 'cultural practices and circumstances of their communities' (Rogoff, 2003: 4).

It can therefore be taken that, as experiences are culturally and individually defined, there can be no truly objective view as each standpoint is exactly that: the world is filtered through individual prior experience and understandings. It can also be argued that this is a liberating view, affording any number of possible world views and allowing for a development of thinking as it is the challenge to an exist-ing view or recognition of alternatives that creates new understandings – a cogni-tive dissonance that propels understanding forward, or as Donaldson argues, the possibility of 'what could be' (Donaldson, 1978: 86). The rejection of universals also means the acceptance that interpretations are temporally and spatially depen-dent; that is, that the time and place will alter the interpretations that anyone has of any given situation. This fact has to be embraced, as the human world does not exist in a vacuum, and to try to sterilize all variables would not be consistent with an interpretivist paradigm in which 'the central endeavour . . . is to understand the subjective world of human experience' (Cohen et al., 2011: 17).

Context cannot therefore be ignored. This point is identified as significant by Habermas (1984) when he argues that 'communicative action is dependent on situational contexts, which represent in turn segments of the life-world of the participants in interaction' (1984: 278). It is supported by Rogoff who states that 'I regard all human activity as embedded in context; there are neither context-free situations nor decontextualized skills' (Rogoff, 1990: 27). This does not mean that skills are not transferable. For example, the skill of swimming could happen in a pool, a lake or the sea, but it has to happen somewhere and each different location contextualizes it. The children in this book are engaged in discussions about films, books and pictures. Both the 'situation' of the children's discussion and the lan-guage that is employed in this process are relevant and important. They are active ingredients as the children construct meaning together. Kumpulainen and Wray (2002) also argue that a sociocultural perspective emphasizes the 'situatedness of thinking and speaking in the context of activity' (p. 18) and extend the notion of context beyond the cultural to include the historical and institutional. This book is built on research that took place in an educational establishment in England in the early 21st century; the experiences of the children in the study are unique in this 'situation' and the 'social interaction and context' are therefore 'not separated from the learning situation' (Kumpulainen and Wray, 2002: 18). The educational and social context of the research is the 'stage' on which the action happens.

Thus far, consideration has been given to the interpretation of 'reality' and how this is socially constructed, as well as consideration of the prior knowledge, both individually and culturally, that agents bring to a meaning-making situational context. The place of language is central to all of this, as the central tool for the *co*-construction of knowledge, a resulting inter-subjectivity or joint understanding between communicators. Kumpulainen and Wray argue that a sociocultural per-spective 'stresses intersubjectivity and the construction of meanings in interaction' (Kumpulainen and Wray, 2002: 26) and Rojas-Drummond and colleagues argue that 'it is through discursive interactions that knowledge is co-constructed and meanings are negotiated and re-negotiated' (2008: 178). It is the co-construction of these joint meanings that lies at the heart of the research undertaken here, as dif-ferent spotlights are turned onto the co-constructive process in action.

Meaning is communicated through language and this occurs within a situational context. Hymes argues that to have a theory of language, the use of language in 'contexts of situation' (1977: 3) should be investigated directly. He identifies what Rojas-Drummond et al. (2006) describe as a 'nesting hierarchy of units of analysis' (p. 88). First and most broadly, there are what Hymes terms 'speech situations'. In this study, the situation has an educational context, more specifically a state-run primary classroom in a small rural town. This will have impacted on the discussions that happened within it, in terms of the children's understandings about the situation of being at school, and their interpretation of who they are engaged with and why. The cultural context will have informed the experiences and knowledge the children bring to their task of co-construction, and can be seen as what is recognized by Todorov as 'extra-linguistic elements' (1982: 9). These contextual features are 'extra' to the actual dialogue that takes place, but influence it. The term 'speech situation' can be usefully re-named *co-constructive situation* to recognize the joint meaning-making context of the classroom, as this is where all the discussions that are explored within the book happen.

Hymes' second unit of analysis is located within the speech situation and relates to the 'speech event' itself. By this, he means the type of communication that is occurring; in this case, the discussions the children engage in which have the goal of co-constructing meaning from text and so the term *co-constructive events* is adopted. Finally, the smallest unit of analysis in Hymes' framework is the 'speech act' or interactional function, which may or may not be verbal (Hymes, 1972: 56). These are the comments or moves made as part of the dialogue itself, which propel the meaning-making process forward. In this research these are termed *co-constructive moves*. By renaming them, the focus on the function of each speech act within the co-constructive process is centralized.

Hymes' focus on communicative events allows him not only to concentrate on the speech between participants but also to analyze the context of talk. He identifies several components of 'event', including participants, mode, shared codes, settings, forms of message and topics and content. This framing helps to identify a multi-levelled picture for analysis, and becomes particularly important when considering dialogue through a sociocultural lens. Hymes' 'situational' context enables consideration of the social and cultural setting, while his recognition of 'event' allows for an acknowledgement of the social process of communication. The analytical framework complements a sociocultural perspective, and if more socio-semiotic considerations are taken then this also allows for a focus on the intended and received meanings of speech. When Mercer (2004) and Mercer and Littleton (2007) describe a sociocultural discourse analysis that looks at intra- and inter-mental processes that feature in dialogue, they place importance on the contextualization of children's talk in addition to considering the psychological and social elements of it. Hymes' work adds a further frame to this tool by considering its context more explicitly.

The central focus of this book is reading as a meaning-making process, a co-constructive comprehension event which necessarily hinges on the interaction between children discussing texts together and also the way they interact with the texts themselves. Thus the engagement with text becomes a situational event in itself, a framework within which interpretations can happen and critical and creative approaches can be encouraged. There are two interactions taking place: one between readers and one between readers and texts. Before turning to consider the dialogic nature of reading, the interaction between readers should be considered in more detail, particularly focusing on the role that talk and dialogue play in the development of thinking.

The role of language in the co-construction of meaning

At the heart of this study is the concept of comprehension as a co-constructive meaning-making process. While an isolated individual can make sense of the world through their own perceptions and experience, creating, or intending meaning, necessarily needs another person because 'meaning is an emergent property of coordinated action' (Gergen, 1999: 145–6). In other words, the ability to mean anything is achieved 'through the supplemental actions of others. The meaning of my words and actions is not fundamentally under my control. I need you to mean anything' (ibid.). There are two slightly different points here. On the one hand, meaning-making can be seen as interpretation, suggesting that all experiences/perceptions are assigned meaning by the 'receiver'. Gergen, on the other hand, is describing meaning-making as the *creation* of meaning to be communicated, suggesting that this cannot happen in a vacuum and must involve a respondent.

Underpinning this theory is the assumption that language is the main tool for the communication of meaning, and that therefore the 'original mode' of language is to reach understanding (Habermas, 1984: 288). The *intended meaning* and the *interpreted meaning* need to correlate for understanding to happen. The nature of that tool then needs exploring, particularly if it gives insight into the oral language use of children. Therefore, the first area of language pertinent to this study is semiotics, and the theories surrounding the structure of language as a system.

Saussure (1983) is taken to be one of the founding fathers of structuralist semiotic theory and in his *Course in General Linguistics* he describes the communication of meaning as the construction and interpretation of 'signs'. The words used to communicate then become the 'signifiers' of the meaning, which is 'signified' (Saussure, 1983). The words themselves, then, are the signifiers of thought and meaning, a relationship that Vygotsky also explores when stating that 'thought is not merely expressed in words; it comes into existence through them' (Vygotsky, 1962: 125). Vygotsky's argument stems from a non-distinguishable difference between the phenomena of thought (or meaning) and language, the point that both are mutually dependent on each other, making it impossible to have one without the other. The very fact an utterance carries meaning makes it a word, otherwise it would just be a sound.

The notion of 'signs' is integral to structuralist and symbolic-interactionist views of language. These perspectives see that words are imbued with intended meaning and interpreted as having meaning. The word becomes the 'signifier' of the meaning of the thought, or the 'signified', and while thought can be expressed in alternative means (musically, for example), there is a fundamental aspect of language that makes it arguably more reliable through its precision as a meaning communicator or 'signifier' (as opposed to, say, musical expression). It invites a response which in turn invites another response which signifies a development of thought and meaning, and this is the central basis for our construction of reality. It could be argued that musical expression also invites a response which in turn could build an idea, but the difference is that language is the system or tool that is most reliably used to communicate and construct meaning. The implication of this, then, is that the more elaborate the vocabulary, the more precise meanings can be, and more nuance of meaning can be specified and understood by both speaker and listener. The notion assumes, however, that one has the vocabulary necessary to signify the meaning as intended, or that perhaps a smaller vocabulary limits the complexity of one's individual or collaborated thoughts. This suggests a view of thinking whereby complexity is not possible with a limited vocabulary, as such thinkers have incomplete linguistic tools to enable them to fully express complicated ideas. Alternatively, perhaps the quality of thought is in the quality of communication, and this need not be overly complex, but it should engage an allowance of understanding for the listener. The best collaborative thinking, then, may depend on the 'match' between speakers and their ability to both communicate their own meaning and understand each other.

The interpretation of signs is not a one-way process; the listener is an active participant in the action for whom the sign must satisfy. The role of the listener is to comprehend and evaluate the sign. Furthermore, they must interpret the probable significance that it has. In his work on interaction, Wells develops this idea. He acknowledges the importance of collaboration, and in particular the listener's role in accessing the cues that are apparent in the signal and matching those with the appropriate past experience. This all happens within the context of the discourse, and ultimately the listener has to decide what it is that the speaker actually meant and assign a meaning to the language (Wells, 1981: 47). The role of the listener is also emphasized by Habermas (1984) who discusses the role of the listener in determining meaning. He referred to speakers as 'S' and hearers as 'H':

> S will only be able to accomplish his criterion of giving rise to a certain meaning (*meinung*) in H if H recognizes this intention and understands what is meant – understands, that is, the meaning of a corresponding symbolic expression. Solely on the basis of knowing *that* S has the intention of achieving understanding, H will not be able to infer what S means and wants to communicate with him [author's emphasis].
>
> *(Habermas, 1984: 275)*

It is not enough to have an understanding of the intention of achieving an understanding. The ability must be to elicit from signs the same meaning with which they were imbued by the speaker. This fundamental assumption links back to

Gergen's writing, that without an implied listener there is no meaning to be made, and further connects to the assumptions that this is a social reality co-constructed from what is communicated and understood. Importantly, this understanding does not happen in a cultural vacuum; all talk is contextualized. As Maybin (1994) argues:

> understandings are constructed between people, through dialogue, and are shaped by the social and cultural context of the interaction. Talk is not a transparent conduit through which knowledge is passed, but an integral part of how understanding is collaboratively accomplished.
>
> *(Maybin, 1994: 132)*

These theorists argue that knowledge is *co-constructed*, not transferred from one person to another. It is the amalgam of intended and interpreted meaning, and the social and cultural context is a key influence on the manner of these intentions and interpretations.

Language as a linear process

The process of language as an exchange of meaning leading to a co-construction or inter-subjectivity can be argued to be a linear one, with each word following the next, not uttered simultaneously. The very term co-construction implies a notion of gradual building and at a word level, this happens one step at a time. It is impossible for one person to utter two words at once, so each word must lead to the next, with an unfolding of intended and interpreted meaning.

This linearity of language and the physical forming of words can slow down the communication, and 'talking around' a subject to try to communicate an idea or to cope with shifting ideas can lead to a lack of coherence. As it is only possible to utter one word at a time, each becomes dependent on the next and a consistent intention of meaning needs to be maintained throughout this process. A 'syntagmatic interdependence' (Saussure, 1983: 121) between what comes before and what follows then emerges, and this context leads to the true construction of meaning as ideas are built upon each other. Words do not operate in isolation and their meaning is dependent on a broader syntactic system in which they occur (Habermas, 1984: 276). The language system, then, needs to be learnt so that language can be used, interpreted and manipulated to make meaning in collaboration, and common rules need to be understood to successfully navigate this territory. Halliday (1993) extends this idea and argues that the essence of learning itself is the learning of meaning, at the heart of which lies language:

> The distinctive feature characteristic of human learning is that it is a process of making meaning – a *semiotic* process; and the prototypical form of human semiotics is language. Hence the ontogenesis of language is at the same time the ontogenesis of learning [Halliday's emphasis].
>
> *(Halliday, 1993: 93)*

However, he argues that language is the 'essential condition of knowing, the process by which experience *becomes* knowledge' (1993: 94), suggesting that there is no learning without language and 'learning *is learning to mean*' [Halliday's emphasis] in a 'language based theory of learning'. This statement limits learning to a language base. Yet, as suggested earlier, meaning derived from other contexts and perceptions may not always be language based. For example, a child soon learns not to pull a cat's tail in a 'once bitten, twice shy' scenario. Notwithstanding this, Halliday's discussion on how language is learnt and developed is useful, especially as he describes the key features of child language development that move from 'acts of meaning', by creating signs, through to the adoption of grammar and more conventional systems.

Language, he argues, is not learnt by expanding a vocabulary of isolated words. Rather it is the relationship of these words to each other that leads to an increased knowledge of the system. This concept can then equally apply to a growing lexicon, which accommodates an increasing nuance of meaning. The growing classification of experiences expands to accommodate language in the same way – or to assimilate new words into existing categories, also resonating with Piaget and his theories of language and child development. However, this additional language is more sophisticated, building a nuance of meaning into each internal modal of the world (Wells, 2009) through increasingly precise vocabulary and understanding of the syntactic system in which it operates. The use of this precise language means a more finely tuned intended meaning, with the impact on interpretation being a closer response to that which has been expressed. For example, describing an object as 'red' affords a number of different interpretations. However, the words 'crimson', 'patent', 'blood' or 'pillar-box' suggest nuances of meaning that bring the associated intended and interpreted meanings closer.

The dialogic nature of talk

The nature of talk is that it implies more than a single voice. Theories around dialogue and the dialogic tend to stem from the work of Bakhtin (1981) who argues that all speech is dialogue, as every utterance has the implication of responding or response, either internal to the mind of the speaker or from a listener. No single speech act can happen in pure isolation as the concept of dialogue suggests that each speech act is part of a chain. Therefore, meanings develop 'not in one utterance but rather in chains of utterances and in longer episodes' (Kumpulainen and Wray, 2002: 25). This idea can be seen as an extension of Saussure's 'interdependent syntagmatism' (1983: 121) which refers to the placement of an utterance between what came before and what follows, in which he is particularly referring to single words. In a development of this concept, Wells defines a 'syntagmatic dimension' of talk, referring to the 'sequential chaining in which one turn follows another' (Wells, 1981: 27), and from this chaining, meaning and understanding are developed. Bakhtin argues that 'understanding and response are dialectically merged and mutually condition each other, one is impossible without the other'

(Bakhtin, 1981: 282). So, even as an utterance is created, there is the consideration of what the response can be: the speaker puts themselves into the position of a listener to make an interpretation of their own words.

The central premise of this book is that primary school-aged children are able to jointly construct meaning through dialogue. The children show that they are engaged with each other, and the co-construction of meaning is an *inter*-mental process (Mercer and Littleton, 2007). Children are able to think together, connecting to each other's thoughts through the communication and understanding of signs that have consistent meaning for both speaker and listener. Even though younger children have a less experienced knowledge of the language system, they are still able to enter into what Vygotsky defines as an 'inter-subjective understanding' between speakers. To explain this idea, he uses an example from the writings of Tolstoy where two people engage in a dialogue and say very little, yet understand each other (Vygotsky, 1962: 237). However, it can be similarly evidenced in talk when speakers finish each other's sentences or enjoy a play on words. To link this argument back to the semiotic theories explored in the last section, the term 'sign' implies that there is a recipient to whom it is directed. Saussure argues that ' . . . in order to have a language there must be a community of speakers . . . a language never exists even for a moment except as a social fact, for it is a semiological phenomenon' (Saussure, 1983: 77). In other words, to pick up on the 'semiological' notion, if language is a system of signs, then these only have meaning if they are recognized as such and interpreted.

These arguments suggest that even the very youngest language users are concerned with response, yet observation of young children talking and playing often shows them involved in a seeming monologue, not concerned with the listener's response at all, and focusing only on their own speech. From a Bakhtinian perspective, even if a child appears to be only engaged with their own idea, perhaps responding to their own previous comment rather than the turn of the previous speaker, there is still a perceived response and interpretation (Barnes and Todd, 1995). The 'inner voice' then acts as a respondent to support the development of the idea.

A dialogic space of possibility

The concept of implied 'response' that has been proposed by theories of dialogue (Bakhtin, 1981) offers a notion of a continual iterative motion of understanding; that is, meanings change as they move back and forth between speakers. Wegerif suggests that there is no clear line between speaker and listener, but rather 'an inclusive space of dialogue within which self and other mutually construct and reconstruct each other' (2008b: 353). This idea of 'dialogic space' is important as it creates a concept of *possibility*, while in the space between speakers – that is, the gap between intention and interpretation – meanings are provisional and response possibilities multiple. Based on what a speaker has said and the meaning interpreted, a number of different responses could be deemed appropriate by the respondent.

Response then propels the possibility of alternative meanings forward again as the dialogic space is re-entered and the provisional meaning negotiated further through the next round of intention and interpretation. This theoretical model illustrates the dualistic nature of meaning-making which is truly collaborative in nature and jointly owned by participants. It is only by engaging and re-engaging in the space between speakers that inter-subjectivity can be negotiated.

The suggestion of a space in which meaning is created and continually restructured is highlighted in the work of Barnes and Todd (1995: 141), who discuss the 'indeterminate' nature of meaning in dialogue and its joint ownership, and Maybin whose research found meanings and understandings to be 'provisional and frequently contested' (1994: 148). From this, she suggests an ambiguity in meaning, in which it is the listener, not the speaker, who chooses an interpretation, changing as the listener becomes the speaker. The space of understanding between the speakers in a dialogue is where the meaning exists and changes, and therefore the meaning and intentions of the speakers cannot be automatically assumed by a third, observing party. As Wells suggested, analysts and participants have differing goals (1981: 70). In listening to children and making claims about the assumptions of their meaning, there lies a problem of interpretation, and potentially 'over'-interpretation, a warning suggested by Edwards and Westgate (1987) in their research.

In another exploration of how meanings are co-constructed and negotiated, Lyle's (1993) research followed children in role-play discussions as they responded to information given on task cards. She found that groups of children talking 'make provisional meanings as they feel their way towards some shared understanding' (1993: 194) and that ' . . . the meanings that children made were not stable, they were fluid and changing, built up from their existing knowledge, the information on the cards, and their own explicit and implicit summaries of their discussions' (1993: 194). Wegerif (2008a, 2008b), Barnes and Todd (1995), Maybin (1994) and Lyle (1993), through different means, all point towards a space between intended and interpreted meaning that is fluid and provisional. Nystrand et al. (1997) suggested that the dialogism of discourse emerges from the tension between one response and the next, using the term 'refract' to describe this tension (1997: 8). The co-construction of meaning then happens across this space of refraction.

The concepts of dialogic space and provisional meaning are central to the themes in this book and so the term *dialogic space of possibility* is presented as a combination of the theories identified above. The term attempts to encompass the notion of meaning existing not quite with either participant in a dialogue, but somewhere between, and therefore always open to change. Littleton and Mercer (2013) describe an 'Inter-mental Creativity Zone' that appears similar, though it relates specifically to interaction between teacher and child. Here the concept of the dialogic space of possibility is an extension of Wegerif's 'dialogic space' and includes and makes reference to the fluid and exploratory potential of the space between speakers.

Dialogical thinking

The concept of 'thinking' as an inter-mental as well as intra-mental process is central to the idea of meaning evolving over several turns of discourse. Paul (1987) extends the idea of the dialogic into his theories on critical thinking, particularly in relation to the dialogue of the inner voice. His suggestion is that the ability to reason and rationalize with oneself is an important feature of developing rational knowledge. It is the consideration of possible opposing arguments and an empathy with the alternative viewpoint that enables the development of rational thinking, through a 'dialogical exchange' (Paul, 1987: 129). This is particularly important if there is no one set to engage an alternative point of view. For Paul, then, the ability to voice other points of view is not only advantageous, but a key skill of rational thinking. He actually proposes the term 'multi-logical' rather than merely 'dialogical' as there may be multiple opposing viewpoints. He also argues that this is a particularly creative way of thinking as it extends the thinker beyond one fixed 'monological' frame of reference with a defined set of logical moves. That is, 'creativity is essential to all rational dialogical thinking, because dialogical thinking is a series of reciprocal creative acts wherein we move up and back in our minds from categorically different imagined roles' (1987: 143).

Paul's theory furthers the argument for considering a dialogic space of possibility between speakers or thinkers, or perhaps just between ideas and responses, whether they involve another person or not. Where he is talking primarily about the skill of being able to interrogate possible responses as an aid to rational thinking, it is his described iterative movement between possible responses that requires a space for 'possibility thinking' (Craft, 2000). However, Paul's theory of dialogical thinking places the emphasis on an opposition or alternative point of view, while the joint construction of knowledge and development of an argument does not necessarily continually highlight opposing or 'multi-logical' thinking. Within a dialogic space of possibility there are opportunities for exploration through the extension of ideas, not necessarily the opposition of them. Paul's theory specifically draws on the concept of voice and implies an ongoing inner dialogue as an essential ingredient in the development of rationalization. The importance he places on empathy and creativity as features of a flexible and rational thinker sets the ability of not just seeing but also constructing other points of view as crucial to critical thinking and the process of comprehending text.

Making meaning from text

At the heart of the reading comprehension processes that are central to this book are two relationships that can be viewed as dialogic in nature. The first is the creation of meaning between text and reader, and the second is the creation of meaning between readers when they comprehend together. However, before exploring these dialogic relationships, the location of reading within a sociocultural framework is proposed, and the notions of 'text' and 'reading' are examined particularly, as the focus of the reading activities analyzed in this book extend beyond written or verbal modes of text.

Text and reading: a multi-modal approach

The RAND Reading Study Group (RRSG) (2002: 11) defined comprehension as 'the process of simultaneously extracting and constructing meaning through inter-action and involvement with written language', and this can be seen as a traditional model of reading comprehension where the emphasis is placed upon the transac-tion of making meaning through the reader's actions. A problem with this defini-tion, however, is that it assumes that reading, writing and text are fixed absolutes, and tied to the verbal or written forms. On the other side of the social semiotic fence, Kress suggests that 'reading is communication' and that communication only happens when there is interpretation (2010: 35), with readers drawing on semiotic, multi-modal resources to make sense. This broadest sense of reading encompasses the suggestion that reading not only includes non-written forms, but can also be applicable to much broader communicative frameworks.

The use of the term 'multi-modal' and what this actually means are increasingly drawing critical response. On one hand, embracing non-print forms of text can be seen as a prerequisite to 21st-century literacy, when the digital, moving-image and other visual modes are prevalent in communicative practice beyond school. For example, Bearne et al. (2007) raise the question of how teaching reading can encompass all text modes that are available and make use of the fact that chil-dren experience many different multi-modal text forms outside school. However, Bazalgette and Buckingham (2013) recommend caution when embracing the term 'multi-modal'. They suggest that, as a label for non-print forms of text, it oversim-plifies the complexity of modes, and is used merely as an opportunity to bring to the classroom text forms that might otherwise be regarded as less valuable than the written word. They also argue that the term 'multi-modal' brings an inappropriate distinction between 'written' and 'other', when in fact printed, written texts have a visual element that makes multi-modal analysis possible (for example, considering font choices or graphic design).

Hassett suggests a combination of sociocultural and semiotic theories of mean-ing-making to consider 'not just a matter of reading the word, but rather, a matter of interpreting and representing meaning across various contexts and audiences with multiple sign systems' (2010: 90). Kress (2003: 141) suggests that we need a theory 'which tells us how to combine meaning derived from writing and from image into a single coherent entity' and Taylor takes the stance that texts 'are seen as multi-modal manifestations of situated meaning with frames or boundaries and comprising properties with cohesive elements' (2012: 160). This idea is useful as it not only supports the notion of multi-modality, but also introduces the idea of framing, which may be physical or implied (after Lotman, 1994: 383), and the fact that there are boundaries to texts. 'Reading', then, becomes the act of making meaning from text, in whatever form it might take.

Most usefully, Hassett argues that traditional models of literacy that fix reading, writing and text can be updated so that 'the text to be understood is a visual text with a variety of modes for making sense. With this change to "text", the reader becomes one who uses the multi-modal resources available to negotiate the text and interactively construct new meaning' (2010: 92). This definition assumes an inclusion of texts with different forms, the emphasis being returned to the reader's action of making sense. The works of Arizpe and Styles (2003), Mackey (2007) and Arizpe (2013) all explore children's responses to visual text forms and highlight the importance of these valid reading sources.

Notwithstanding this, it is important to recognize that different text types afford alternative approaches to making meaning, and readers may negotiate them differently. One of the key differences between writing and image relates back to the earlier discussion about the linearity of language. In writing, as each word leads to the next, there is a specified temporal reading pathway. The texts can therefore be called 'linear' and this has an impact on the emergence of the meaning derived. Images, on the other hand, afford alternative spatial pathways of reading as the elements of image are 'simultaneously present' (Kress, 2003: 20). This suggests more interpretations as the image 'offers possibilities to the viewer for the establishing of relations between elements in the representation, which in the syntax of speech or writing are fully pre-given' (2003: 166). The texts can therefore be called 'spatial' as the reader can choose how they navigate the space of the image. Barthes suggests that this does not mean that a totally random or 'anarchic' approach to reading an image ensues. These are still texts situated in a cultural context that may lend themselves to being interpreted in a particular way (Barthes, 1977: 46). For example, an image interpreted by someone who is familiar with a left-top to bottom-right written language form may automatically be drawn to concentrate on the left-hand side of a picture first.

The approach that is taken to start to make sense of a visual image is steeped in the experiences each reader brings with them, whether they are personal, cultural or both. Potentially, this multiplicity of possible meanings might invite more discussion around an image than a written text, suggesting that the use of images in engaging children in text comprehension can support their disposition to search for meaning and explore possibilities. It can also support children to engage with meanings beyond the literal, rather than being satisfied with the successful decoding of words. With the absence of a 'right answer', children are then pushed to justify their reasoning and accept alternatives. They must engage in the critical-thinking process. By offering children the chance to engage dialogically with ambiguous text, the dialogic space of possibility is extended as the readers creatively engage in the process of generating meaning.

Kress and van Leeuwen (1996) explore the difference between linear and spatial texts by describing their structure and resulting reading pathway engagement in terms of syntagmatics and paradigmatics, which relates back to the work of Wells (1981). They suggest that linear texts impose the sequence of, and the connection between, the elements, as one item must precede the next. This is a syntagmatic relationship. Alternatively, spatial texts are paradigmatic as the relationship between elements may 'follow a certain paradigmatic logic . . . but leave it to the reader to sequence and connect them' (Kress and van Leeuwen, 1996: 223). This offers an interesting consideration when regarding responses to animated moving-image texts. They are at once temporal and spatial, with the 'action' in any frame direct-ing the paradigmatic dimension, but the sequence of frames dictating the syn-tagmatic relationship. Kress and van Leeuwen reinforce this by arguing that the more coherent influence is temporal, with the spatial and compositional element enhancing the linear (1996: 242).

These arguments all lead to a view of reading that necessarily includes more than just written forms of text, and all of the texts the children encountered within this study involved some visual image, whether in animated films, picturebooks or still images. The stance taken in this book is a practical application of the arguments above. When trying to understand the process of making meaning as a dialogic interaction between texts and readers, it is not desirable to impose the limitations of the written word and the potential barriers this might include. By drawing on a wider sense of text, and focusing on the transaction of meaning-making itself, it is possible to come closer to the 'single coherent entity' that Kress (2003: 141) suggests.

A sociocultural view of reading

The comprehensive National Reading Panel (NRP) research in 2002 draws on Durkin (1993) to observe that 'comprehension has come to be viewed as the essence of reading' (cited in NRP, 2002: 4). The role of the 'reader', then, is to deduce and infer meaning from text, and all they can bring to the reading event is the sum of their experiences so far, or rather their world schema or internal model of the world (Wells, 2009). These ideas relate entirely back to the initial arguments about meaning-making explored earlier. At that point it was suggested that chil-dren engage with the world and make meaning from it, viewing, perhaps, reality as the largest text possible. In its broadest sense, then, reading is 'making sense of the world around me' (Kress, 2003: 140). Kress also argues that both situations are ones of interpreting signs and on a smaller and more tangible scale, the way that children read the texts they have been given is the same process. A further link can be established by applying the work of Hymes (1972) who identifies communica-tive situations, events and acts. It is possible to define a hierarchy of reading analysis using Hymes' communicative hierarchy in terms of reading situation (for these children, an education context), reading event (the task of making meaning from the texts) and reading acts (the specific text comprehension strategies that the chil-dren use). From a sociocultural perspective, the context and situation of the event inform the acts. To make meaning, we must draw on our existing knowledge of the world, or schema.

Schema theory pervades the theoretical literature on reading comprehen-sion, and was particularly prevalent in the 1980s. Smith describes the process of

comprehension as 'relating relevant aspects of the world around us – written language in the case of reading – to the intentions, knowledge, and expectations we
have in our heads' (1988: 6) and Anderson and Pearson (1984) posit that all reading
comprehension is necessarily grounded in the reader's schema:

> Whether we are aware of it or not, it is this interaction of new information
> with old knowledge that we mean when we use the term comprehension.
> To say that one has comprehended a text is to say that she has found a mental
> 'home' for the information in the text, or else that she has modified an exist-
> ing mental home in order to accommodate the new information.
>
> *(Anderson and Pearson, 1984: 255)*

The seminal work of Palincsar and Brown (1984) clarifies this further by suggesting
that the factors producing comprehension are the 'compatibility' between the text
content and the reader's knowledge, and the strategies employed by readers to
'enhance understanding'. They suggest that there is an overlap between the prior
knowledge of the reader and the text content (1984: 117); in other words, there
has to be a connection, or perhaps a match, between what is known and what
is read. This 'match' links to the notion in the previous section about speakers
needing at least some common ground to be able to respond to each other, and
supports the idea of a dialogic transaction between reader and text. Comprehension
is not viewed as passive, but rather necessitating an active engagement with reading
situation and event, with the author and with other readers. Pardo (2004) argues:

> A common definition for teachers might be that comprehension is a process
> in which readers construct meaning by interacting with text through the
> combination of prior experience, information in the text, and the stance the
> reader takes in relationship to the text.
>
> *(Pardo, 2004: 272)*

Pardo's view highlights the 'situational' aspect of reading, with the only static
element being the text itself; the reader, their experience and their stance are in a
changing and evolving state. A similar view of reading is taken by Snow and Sweet,
who argue that the three elements of comprehension are the text, the reader and
the activity. However, they argue that these three elements are all influenced by the
sociocultural context of the reading situation and that this needs to be constantly
kept in mind while making use of research about reading (Snow and Sweet, 2003: 2).
Even the positioning of 'text' as a stable element is now less secure with the increase
of text modes that allow for text modification by the reader. Story 'apps' where the
reader might contribute to the text itself by drawing images or otherwise change it
during the process of reading challenge the model of text as a fixed entity.

   In considering the prior knowledge that readers use to construct meaning from
text, however, there is an issue about the relevance of the information accessed,
and this relates to both written and visual texts. Pressley (2000) refers to theories

that suggest: 'one of the ways that weak readers undermine their comprehension is by relating to texts they are reading prior knowledge that is not directly relevant to the most important ideas in the text, making unwarranted and unnecessary inferences as they do so' (2000: 550). He is referring specifically to the reader of the written word here, and the notion of the 'weak reader' seems to particularly identify children who struggle to both decode at the level of individual words and make meaning from the whole. However, if this notion is applied to the reading of images or visuals, it becomes problematic. If some prior knowledge is viewed as more relevant to the reading event than other knowledge, there is a suggestion of a 'correct answer' and qualification of the ideas that meaning-makers have. In other words, the idea of an open construction of meaning is reduced if ultimately the 'most important ideas in the text' must be accessed. Hassett's (2010) argument is that we must accept that there are always multiple meanings, and that each reader must create their own larger meanings, as each text adds to their understanding of themselves and the world. Seen socioculturally, each reading event adds to the stock of 'prior knowledge' a reader has and informs the next 'text'.

This can be an issue for teachers, however. Dombey (2010: 111) identifies the tension between supporting children to make 'unforeseen meanings from what they read, while striving to ensure that these meanings are answerable to the text'. She suggests that: 'teachers should be encouraged to be both more adventurous and trusting of their students' capacity to engage with important issues and challenging ideas' (2010: 118). Other writers have also explored this issue of genuine meanings being created between reader and text, challenging the notion of a teacher-prescribed, pre-ordained, correct response, and arguing for an approach to literacy teaching that automatically assumes a 'proliferation of meanings' (Damico et al., 2009: 178). Swain (2010) found that it was important for teachers to prompt open-ended discussions to enable children to reach their own meanings. Consequently, if comprehension is viewed as 'thinking that is a dynamic and continuous process of thought, rather than a series of pre-packaged skills' (Smith, 2010: 66), then it is the teacher's role to model and celebrate such behaviours and to offer rich and varied literacy experiences for children, while also modelling the critical metacognitive skills that that allow creative thinkers to monitor their own understanding and decide what is reasonable. Without experiencing situations that invite multiple interpretations, children are not encouraged to look beyond the most simplistic interpretation, and are geared towards searching for the 'right answer' only, without exploring possibilities. By making the process a social and dialogic one, the self-monitoring, critical-thinking processes that are part of deciding what prior knowledge is appropriate to use to infer meaning are checked by the process of negotiating the meaning of the text with someone else.

A dialogic view of reading

Lotman (1994) broadly defines text as having two functions; the first a 'transmission of information' and the second 'the generation of new meanings' (Leo and

Mandelker, 1994: 377). Based on the second function, the process of meaning-making implies that the 'reading' of text is automatically a dialogic process, with the two parties being author and reader. The difference from an oral dialogue, of course, is that the two parties are separated by time and space, making each reading event unique in situation. This affords polysemic possibilities, an idea that is developed by Barthes in his consideration of text. He suggests that from the initial intended meaning by the creator, 'as soon as the text is conceived as a polysemic space where the paths of several possible meanings intersect, it is necessary to cast off the monological, legal status of signification, and pluralize it' (Barthes, 1981: 37). There is a strong link here to the nature of dialogic and inter-mental thinking suggested previously. If the initiation of a dialogue is also seen as the creation of text by an author, then a dialogic reply can be taken as the reader's response. The dialogic space between these events can be interpreted as Barthes' 'polysemic space', the point at which many possible interpretations exist, thus making it a dialogic space of possibility. While the text cannot literally respond to the reader, it exists as a springboard or prompt for the reader's response. Furthermore, a reader engaging in dialogical thinking (Paul, 1987) offers their own alternatives and different, potentially multiple, interpretations of the texts to which they are responding. The reader can enter into a dialogue where they supply the implied response from the text by asking questions of it, hypothesizing and wondering what its intended meaning is. In the same way that Donaldson describes the process of learning as 'grappling' with the world (1978), so the reader grapples with the text to make sense of it, bringing their own past experiences to support them.

Rosenblatt's (1978) seminal work highlights the importance of the 'transaction' between reader and text, recognizing that the reader brings with them their own experiences, expectations and motivations which affect the meaning that is constructed, making reading a situational event. A sociocultural perspective on reading not only incorporates the transactions between text and readers, but also recognizes the context of the reading activity, which is affected by time and place, and the variables in readership (RRSG, 2002), which relate to the reader's prior knowledge, motivation and experience. These are the influences that allow readers to fill gaps of meaning in the text (Iser, 1978) as the heart of meaning-making from this perspective 'lies at the intersection of reader, text and context' (Pearson, 2009: 19). As a result, meanings are not fixed, but fluid and situational, created by readers who draw on their prior experiences, ask questions, evoke images and make predictions to comprehend (Palincsar and Brown, 1984; Keene and Zimmerman, 1997; Pressley, 2006). Smith (2010: 66) picks up the concept of a space between text and reader by describing the process as one in which readers import new text into an 'imaginative space' where thinking takes place. She describes this metaphorical space as filled with ideas, expressions and prior experiences, 'emotive, experiential, inter-textual' baggage, and calls it an interpretive framework. By conceiving of this space as one of dialogic possibility, the idea is expanded and the implications of it are less fixed. It is not just about drawing on what is known, but also the possibility of what could be.

The relationship between readers

The relationship between the text and the reader is not the only dialogic dimension possible. When readers make meaning together, and draw on each other's ideas and experiences to engage with the text, they engage in a dialogic transaction with each other. Taking a sociolinguistic perspective and concentrating on the interaction between texts and readers, rather than context, Bloome and Greene (1984) define this more specifically to suggest that reading can be seen to support social relations between people as they jointly make meaning. The event then includes both interpersonal and intrapersonal processes within the sociocultural context. This involves the individual's own past experiences and approach to the task, as well as their skills and knowledge (the intrapersonal). It also involves the relationship and interaction of the individuals working together in a reading event, and how they organize their joint approach (the interpersonal). Bloome and Greene propose that a sociolinguistic perspective would be concerned primarily with the latter, the interpersonal, yet while the interpersonal relates to the co-construction of meaning, the intrapersonal context is permeated with the cultural influences that affect the individual schema the children bring to the event. The two contexts cannot be entirely separated as each affects the other. For example, it is important that both participants in the event understand each other's references to wider culture as they work together to make meaning; they must both be able to draw on their existing world experience (or schema) and to relate it to the ideas of the other person. This matching of peers has been discussed earlier, but also links to Vygotsky's theory of the Zone of Proximal Development (1978). A 'model' that is too far removed from the learner's experience is not accessible to them to develop their own understanding. Similarly, the 'match' that Palincsar and Brown (1984) describe between text and readers allows for a dialogic space of possibility.

This brings us back to the considerations at the start of the chapter. We make meaning together in a social world and language is the tool for this interthinking. The affordance of talking together is the possibility of meaning-making that draws on the combination of multiple world views. By applying this theory to our understanding of reading comprehension, it makes sense that we should encourage children to make meaning together, to take advantage of the social world of children's learning (Pollard, 1996) and the space between speakers and text. If we view reading as a dialogic enterprise, then we necessarily include the potential of creative meaning-making and the importance of language in this process.

The study

Setting the context

To return to Hymes' (1972) communicative theory, the concept that the interpretation of any present reality is affected by its sociocultural context is congruent with the concept of 'reading' as a situational event. The 'reading of reality' is, then, a necessarily subjective experience. As a person's experiences change and widen, their interpretation of the situations they are in can be viewed through more complex lenses. Cohen et al. (2011) suggest that: 'the principle concern [of interpretive research] is with an understanding of the way in which the individual creates, modifies and interprets the world in which he or she finds himself or herself' (2011: 6). This places the focus on the process of interpretation, rather than the search for an ultimate truth, or truths. The research in this book was conducted as a case study, focusing on the interpretation of language to make meaning. It is 'an enquiry carried out in order to understand' (Bassey, 1999) and deals with what Stake (1995: 8) calls 'particularization'. To explain the location of the research necessitates a further return to Hymes and his nested hierarchy.

The co-constructive situation

The research took place in a one-form entry primary school in the west of England. Children from two classes were selected to represent a range of ages within the school, namely 6-year-olds and 11-year-olds. However, it was important not to draw comparative conclusions from the differing discussions that the children had, as these were snippets in time, rather than a larger longitudinal study. The school was one where there were already well-established relationships with the staff, so the activities that were recorded were part of the normal classroom curriculum. Having an extra adult in the classroom was not unusual for these children and a lead-in time of six months was used where I regularly visited the classes and worked with them. The situation of this talk is therefore educational, and this is reflected in the way that the children talk to each other and how they engage in the task. In a discussion with some Year 6 children about their thoughts on the activity, they admitted that had they not been taking part in the activity as a directed task they would have probably moved on to talk about something else much sooner, abandoning the discussion about the text. They appreciated that this was educational dialogue, and as such was based in the situation of the classroom.

The co-constructive events

Pairs of children were recorded as they discussed a variety of texts. These discussions were not teacher led, though the children were used to 'making sense' of pictures, animated films and picturebooks through discussion, and were guided by the understanding that they should talk about their ideas. They had been taught to ask questions about texts. In this way, the activity was transparent. They were aware that this was a co-constructive task, and that they should work together. However, explicit rules for engagement had not been set. Mercer (2004) acknowledges that taking a qualitative approach to discourse analysis often means a small data set and this does create issues around reliability. In this study the steps taken to address this were to keep the selection of children as open as possible, by involving the class teachers and by being transparent about the research process with the children, so that they knew if and when they were to be videoed and had a choice in this. The confidence with which the children engage in the task is not related to their age; the two classes were equally keen to enjoy the experience, and this is evident through the video vignette data. The children in the vignettes were 'typical' of the children in their particular class, and chose to work together. They were neither the least nor most able children as defined by each class teacher, and as the particular case study children were being recorded, other equally interesting paired discussions were happening with the other children. The children in the vignettes form a representative sample of the class. The vignettes, then, capture a snapshot of how children talk together in the context of a task related to making meaning from texts, in a normal classroom situation.

The co-constructive acts

The videos of the children were transcribed and each turn of dialogue was analyzed to code the functions of the co-constructive acts. The reliability of the data collection occurred through a continual iteration between the video and transcript data. However, this assumed that what was represented is a true record of what was said. This was at times problematic, in particular with the younger children whose voices were less clear. As well as numerous colleagues and students who have seen the recordings and commented helpfully on them, a small group of four reviewers, all with experience of listening to the voices of young children, were given the task of watching the video and reviewing the transcripts. Ultimately, individual words that were problematic to decipher did not alter the coding of co-constructive functions in the dialogues, and so did not bias the data.

A 'constant comparative' (Glaser and Strauss, 1967) inductive approach was used when coding, which enabled a continual iteration between emergent theories and the coding. Thus, the categories for coding were 'generated through the analysis' and were 'outcomes, not prior assumptions brought in to sort the data' (Mercer, 2004: 142). Qualitative data handling software was used to code systematically and these codes were verified by the reviewers. They were presented with the coding schedule and each watched the video and coded samples of the pilot transcripts independently before meeting to discuss the coding and any disparities. A danger with researchers interpreting the meanings in children's talk, highlighted by Edwards and Westgate (1987), is the problem of possibly assigning meaning to utterances that are not intended by the speakers themselves, particularly if these meanings are 'drawn from a significantly different frame of reference' (Edwards and Westgate, 1987: 100). While to some degree this is inevitable, particularly if a social-constructionist perspective is taken, and as the frames of reference between the children and teacher-researcher are necessarily different, the four reviewers helped to triangulate the analysis at this level by agreeing and discussing the data.

The vignettes

Each of the vignettes constitutes a small case, unique in its entirety and analyzed closely to illuminate the linguistic, cognitive and social processes that the children are engaged in. The term 'vignette' is an adaptation of the term as defined by Stenhouse, who uses it to describe a 'sketch' that 'crystallizes some important aspect of the case' (1988: 52) as a style of reporting. In this thesis it refers to data, i.e. to each of the complete dialogues between the children captured on video. They each form a separate moment and complete mini case, and the term 'vignette' has been used to capture the uniqueness of each one.

The classroom discussions that are reported give some insights into the particular cases of each pair of children and the dialogic processes in which they were engaged. The study of children's responses to picturebooks in Arizpe's and Styles' (2003) account sets a clear precedent for the value of looking so closely at individual children, and learning from these observations. Rather than trying to set generalizations from these vignettes, they are used as illustrations and hopefully as prompts for further enquiry and considerations of how we might, as teachers, support and develop this creative discourse, and how important it is to listen to what our children say.

This book reports the discussions from four pairs of children from the Year 1 class (6-year-olds). The Y1 children engaged with either pictures or animated film. The texts were chosen as ones that might stimulate discussion, but deliberately as non-verbal texts so that the children's meaning-making would not be impeded by their word recognition skills or lack thereof. The first pair, Harry and Ben, were videoed engaging with two different pictures. *The Lady of Shalott* by Waterhouse (1888) depicts a woman sitting in a boat on water, with her regalia around her. A tapestry hangs over the side of the boat, trailing in the water. The boat is set amongst reeds on a river with trees behind. *Rene Golconde* by Magritte (1953) depicts a landscape of buildings with uniform windows with blue sky above. There are multiple figures suspended in the air, all wearing bowler hats and coats. Harry and Ben formed the heart of the study and their responses enabled the initial coding scheme. Their discussions are included as two separate vignettes.

The other Y1 vignettes include Hannah and Anna who also discussed the Waterhouse painting and Bella and Georgia who discuss a Klee painting, *They're Biting* (1920), an abstract piece of art which is a line drawing of some figures fishing. The children were not told the titles of the paintings. Liam and James, the final Y1 pairing, discussed the animated film *Otherwise* (Schindler, 2002) from the British Film Institute *Starting Stories* collection (2002). In this narrative, three chameleons find a lizard in their midst and ostracize him. An encounter with an eagle leads to one of the chameleons being captured; the lizard saves the day and they all become friends.

Also included are three pairings from the Y6 class: Sophie and Gina discussed the Magritte painting; Tilly and Kate and Alex and Sam discussed the picturebook

Way Home (Hathorn and Rogers, 1994). The story follows the journey of a boy back to his home. On the way he rescues a kitten from a tree and is chased by an angry dog and an angrier gang of boys. The twist at the end of the story reveals him to be homeless but cosy in a den made of boxes and rubble. However, this conclusion is apparent only from the pictures in the book; the written text simply says, 'Here we are, we're home!' The children who discussed this text were fluent readers and able to decode the written text with ease.

The texts included those with spatial reading pathways and those with temporal reading pathways (Kress, 2003; Barthes, 1977), but all had the potential for narrative comprehension. The mix was deliberate and ultimately the texts served as a springboard for a co-constructive dialogue. However, there is a difference in the way that the children interacted with the texts that should be acknowledged. With the picturebook and animated film, the discussion that the children had followed their initial viewing/reading of the text. With *Otherwise* this was because the whole class watched the animated film together, then they worked in pairs to discuss it. With *Way Home*, both pairs of children read the book silently together then started to talk about it as they reached the final page. This meant that the children had longer to form an independent opinion about the text's meaning before engaging in co-constructive talk. In contrast, in the vignettes where the children were co-constructing meaning from a picture, the response to the text happened as they were experiencing it together. This difference is less noticeable in the *Way Home* vignettes, because the children discussed possibilities for explanations for the text. They had the book in front of them and reviewed pages to further their discussion. In the *Otherwise* vignette, the children engaged in more of a retelling of the narrative rather than creatively finding solutions to its meaning. This may in part be due to the nature of the text which already had a narrative structure, although in *Otherwise* this is only visually and musically presented and there are no words. Even with this in mind, the chains of dialogue, the co-constructive moves and the way that the children jointly negotiated the task are all equally interesting in these three vignettes, and they form an important part of the whole set.

Analyzing the dialogue

To build a picture of the dialogic processes involved in reading together, the data are analyzed on five levels. When discussing the methodology of sociocultural discourse analysis, Mercer (2004) defines it as 'less focused on the language itself and more on its functions for the pursuit of joint intellectual activity' (2004: 141). Here, the sociocultural influences on the discussion are seen as an essential feature of the meaning-making process. However, by considering the dialogic processes explicitly, this analysis allows a deepened exploration of the way that children use co-constructive moves in speech to propel their meaning-making further, particularly by considering a dialogic space of possibility that is afforded by certain moves.

The first level of analysis (which is discussed in the next chapter) considers the language of the dialogic transaction between readers. It is a linguistic and dialogic analysis of the speech acts, a careful coding of the transcript, assigning each speech act a code dependent on its dialogic, co-constructive function. The term 'co-constructive move' relates to the speech moves that propel the co-construction of meaning. The videos of the children talking were transcribed and each turn of the dialogue was considered as a unique co-constructive move. The 'constant comparative' approach taken to coding led to a gradual emergence of ten different codes that reflected particular functions in the task of co-construction. As the analysis progressed, it became evident that some turns in the exchange included more than one co-constructive move, so these were also coded. The data were then considered as a series of connected turns of speech which were termed *dialogic chains of thinking* to reflect the connectedness of each move. This organization of the data led to a dialogic analysis that demonstrated the movement of ideas between speakers and the number of exchanges related to one idea stemming from an initiating comment. Wells (1981) discusses 'sequential chaining' (1981: 27) of speech turns, and here this is extended to incorporate an inter-mental and co-constructive element.

In the second level of analysis (which is detailed in Chapter 4), the language of the dialogue is considered specifically as an indicator of the critical and creative thinking occurring during the dialogic reading process. Sometimes this is at an intra-mental level and relates to the particular speaker's own thinking, but often the inter-thinking (Littleton and Mercer, 2013) is the focus, with the children reading critically and creatively together. The focus is on the ways that the children use language as a tool for this thinking, and how each enables the other to move the meaning forward.

So far the concentration has been on the dialogic process between the readers, but the third level of analysis examines the dialogic transaction between readers and text, considering the specific comprehension strategies the children use as they entangle themselves with the text and how they use these strategies together. The analysis draws on the schema or mental image of the world (Wells, 2009) that the children bring to the reading event, but that exists beyond the 'frame' of the text (physical or implied frame, after Lotman, 1994). In particular it considers the narratives that the children construct to make meaning from the text, and how they engage with it by empathizing and entering the world of the text through imagination and creative thinking.

Crucial to comprehension and also a key thinking skill is self-monitoring; that is, checking one's own understanding of the task at hand. The fourth analytical level examines the importance of metacognition and the children's awareness of the process that is demonstrated as they discuss the texts. Certain linguistic markers demonstrate the children's awareness of the process of their task or speech/reading event, and their motivation to engage in it and with their partner. This is an analysis not just of the 'interaction frame' (Barnes and Todd, 1995: 145), but also of the children's participation as conscious agents of their task progression.

Finally, the fifth level of analysis focuses on the social interaction between the participants and how this is evidenced through what they say. Patterns of language are considered as well as any overt gestures that were interpreted as adding to the co-construction. This level of analysis adds to the initial linguistic and dialogic level as it demonstrates when the co-construction of meaning is truly collaborative and where the children are in fact relating only to their own previous ideas, rather than engaging with the other speaker. It also explores the way that the children use provisional or hypothetical language to maintain a social harmony in the course of their discussion.

In these latter two levels of analysis, it is the structure of the discussion and how it is managed that is in the spotlight. Wells (1981) draws attention to 'chaining' as the connection between turns in dialogue and these two levels of analysis highlight the children's awareness of this, and the steps they take to maintain a smooth progression to a satisfactory task conclusion. In this dialogic approach to understanding reading comprehension, the recognition of children as task managers sets the reading event within a dialogic situation, where learning is not just dictated by the teacher but owned and managed by the children as they undertake tasks together.

Ethical considerations

As with all responsible social sciences research, the study undertaken here was subject to strict ethical considerations and it fell within the bounds defined in the British Education Research Association Guidelines (2011). Moreover, the children in the study were very openly informed about its intent and were included in discussions, for example about where to set up the camera, and in some cases they reviewed the data. They knew that I was interested in the way that they talked together, and were keen to be involved. While the activities in themselves were part of an everyday classroom experience, the collection of data and the dissemination of findings were not, so I sought not only their parent's consent for them to be included but also their own consent, talking with them about my intentions and the outcomes for the research. Additionally, I did not record early sessions with the children, nor take notes; rather, I established myself within the classroom as an extra teacher. Having a primary teaching background helped me to engage with them, and as the two class teachers had similar teaching styles to mine, fitting into the life of the class was easy. I made sure that between sessions the teachers checked with the children to ensure that they were still happy about being included, and the teachers acted as gatekeepers of the research. The children are anonymized in the book, though Harry, Ben, Anna and Hannah keep their first names, largely because they featured in another later study, had reviewed all the research data (declaring their Y1 ideas as 'wacky') and were keen to be acknowledged. As their conversations have intrigued me for several years, this personalization felt important.

Transcription and body language

A simple approach has been taken to the transcription of the dialogue (following Mercer and Littleton, 2007). Each 'turn' of the dialogue is given a new line and standard punctuation is used to denote tone of voice. Where pauses occur they are denoted by ellipses, and simultaneous speech is indicated by square brackets. Gestures that add to the meaning of the dialogue are parenthesized in brackets and italicized. Where words are not clearly transcribed, an explanation (unclear) is included in parentheses.

In Tannen's (1989) notes on transcription, she argues that it is not useful to represent words in their reduced form (for example, 'mighta', 'gonna') to indicate how they were actually said (1989: 202). Her argument stems from the fact that it is difficult to be consistent with non-standard spelling, and that inclusion of such non-standardizations influences the reader in their assumptions about speakers. This research takes a different approach, and uses non-standard spellings to represent words as they were spoken by the children, for two main reasons. First, spoken language is different from written language and to try to standardize it into an acceptable written form would misrepresent the speech. Second, the richness and complexity of the language that has been captured through transcription is embraced. There are inconsistencies in the transcription of words, but the emphasis of the study is on the words as signifiers of meaning and the co-constructive functions they serve, so this is not problematic.

An advantage of collecting video data is the ability to watch as well as hear what occurs. This is not a study of body language communication, though clearly the children's proximity to each other and their eye contact with each other might say something about their ease of working together. Similarly, the animation of their gestures might be seen as an indicator of their enthusiasm for the task – and each other. There are times when the children glance towards the camera, for example, displaying an awareness of the task and the context of the discussion. These factors are not hidden and are commented on when they are relevant to the analysis. The context of this dialogic reading event is that it is a task set by a teacher, within the environment of a classroom.

Chapter summary

Starting from an assumption that children are active agents in their world, and that they make meaning both holistically and narratively, the theories discussed in this chapter situate all meaning in a social and cultural context which is ever-changing and therefore unique. The chapter has argued that language can be viewed as a semiotic system through which meaning is made. Both the speaker and listener play a role in this process, with signified meaning dependent on interpretation. This meaning is fluid and changeable, and exists in the dialogic space between speakers. It may be built from more than the immediate exchange of speech, connecting back to far earlier comments, and even a seeming 'monologue' has the implication of response, so is dialogic. Reflective reasoning considers alternatives and different perspectives and is also therefore dialogical. As a social mode of thinking, co-constructive talk is hypothetical or 'potentiating', with a dialogic space of possibility existing between speakers.

Considering reading, the essence of comprehension as 'meaning-making' was argued and the nature of text explored. Different text modes offer reading pathways for comprehension that may be linear or spatial, and these afford the possibility of multiple interpretations, not least because reading events are unique, situational and interactive occurrences. The author/creator and reader/responder enter into a dialogue separated by space and time. The single reader can provide a response by thinking dialogically and assuming different viewpoints, or considering alternative perspectives. Additionally, a further relationship between two readers/responders making sense of a text together exists, resulting in an inter and intrapersonal experience. From this comes the central proposal: that reading comprehension can be viewed as a dialogic process between readers and text. This is an important concept as it centralizes the space of meaning-making as the key. Clearly, then, what teachers do is crucial, as they can either set up reading experiences that enable children to explore this space in collaboration with each other, thus developing a creative mindset geared towards 'possibility', or they can minimize the potential by setting up activities that are more monologic (Lyle, 2008), where children answer questions about the text but do not own the process of comprehending it.

Finally, the context of the study that illuminates this dialogic perspective on reading visual texts was outlined, with an introduction to the children themselves, the texts that they read and the levels of analysis that will be used to unpack their talking, thinking and responses.

3

TALKING TOGETHER

The language of co-construction

After setting a theoretical basis for the study and considering the general nature of language as a social tool for meaning-making, this chapter now looks in detail at the functions of the language the children in the study use as they co-construct meaning from text. It focuses on the role of speech moves (called co-constructive moves) in generating and maintaining discussion and how, while these might be typified by particular language indicators, their importance lies in their function rather than the exact words used. Ten different coded co-constructive moves are identified in the vignettes of the children's talk and their use is compared across the two vignettes of Harry and Ben.

The chapter analyzes the 'paradigmatic dimension' of dialogue (Wells, 1981: 27), or rather the choices speakers have as to the type of response they make, and how that might affect the language they use. Taking the vignettes as whole discussions, the concept of a dialogic space between speakers is expanded and the affordance of different response moves to open or close the conversation is explored. Moves that open the dialogue and offer possibilities for discussion are regarded as divergent moves, and those that close the dialogue by offering little affordance for continued co-construction are regarded as convergent moves.

Different modes of talk

Many writers have specifically defined modes of talk that are apparent in educational contexts. In particular, the works of Phillips (1985), Fisher (1993), Barnes and Todd (1995), Lyle (1993, 2002), Mercer (1995, 1996, 2000, 2004), Mercer et al. (1999), Mercer and Littleton (2007) and Rojas-Drummond et al. (2006) provide useful and informative frameworks for categorizing the modes of talk employed in a classroom setting where children are talking together. They also all advocate an educational approach that provides opportunities for children to collaborate and use talk in this way.

Barnes and Todd sit at the base of this strand of research with their work which began in the 1970s, investigating the approaches children take to making meaning through talk. They suggest that talk is an opportunity for flexible thinking and being responsive to the suggestions or doubts of others, and that children can 'collaborate in shaping meanings they could not hope to reach alone' (1995: 15). Furthermore, they discuss a mode of talk they call 'exploratory' and acknowledge that the type of talk children will engage in when they are 'outside the visible control of the teacher' (Mercer, 1995: 362) allows them to be flexible and open in their language use. They describe the exploratory mode of talk as including ' . . . hesitations and changes of direction; tentativeness; assertions and questions in a hypothetical modality that invite modification and surmise; self-monitoring and reflexivity' (Barnes and Todd, 1995: 9).

The dialogic space of possibility is central to this mode of talk, as it provides a virtual and cognitive frame for such 'hypothetical modality'. For children to be able to put forward ideas and to explore possibilities and potential solutions, the space for exploration must be created through the language the children use. In extension to this, Phillips' (1985) theory on interactional modes suggests that markers indicate the style of discourse in which children are engaged. Specifically, his research concerns children over the age of nine, and provides an overarching model of analysis. In addition to a hypothetical mode, he identifies four further different modes of talk: experiential, argumentational, operational and expositional. In fact, all of these modes could be deemed as elements of the larger set of features apparent in the Barnes and Todd definition of exploratory talk, but Phillips usefully identifies clear 'mode markers' which indicate the mode of talk. The inclusion of the expositional mode is particularly interesting with regard to the co-construction of meaning from visual text. In Philips' research this mode was less common than others, but here the task encourages it, so a close analysis of how children manage expositional talk can be achieved. The expositional mode is evidenced by the use of questions such as 'where', 'why', 'what' and 'how'. These questions can be seen to determine the content of the response given and open a dialogic space of possibility. If it is true that the exposition mode features less frequently in the language the children use generally (as suggested by Phillips' research), yet could indicate an important entry point to a state of 'possibility thinking' (Craft, 2000), then there are of course implications about the importance of children's expositional questions as triggers for co-constructive thinking.

Fisher highlights the value of talk 'which features argument and exploration through hypothesis and challenge' (1993: 240) as she recognizes that discussions where children quickly agree with each other finish very quickly. In other words, there is no space or possibility for them to generate new thinking. However, children engaging in talk together are able to engage in solving genuine problems, rather than being tested for the *right* answer. It is not enough to merely suppose that genuine problem-solving through the use of an exploratory mode of talk is beneficial; a close analysis of how this actually happens gives a greater insight not only into the ways that children talk together, but also how they negotiate the route through provisional meanings to a joint understanding.

Mercer (1995) weaves the strands created by Barnes and Todd, Phillips, Lyle and Fisher to further the debate around the types of talk most useful in 'constructing knowledge'. His concern lies with the quality of talk and his categories for modes of talk reflect this. Ultimately, he describes a 'kind of talk which is good for solving intellectual problems and advanced understanding' thus:

> First it is a kind of talk in which partners present ideas as clearly and as explicitly as necessary for them to become shared and jointly evaluated. Second, it is talk in which partners *reason* together – problems are jointly analyzed, possible explanations are compared, joint decisions are reached. From an observer's point of view their reasoning is *visible* in the talk [Mercer's emphasis].
>
> *(Mercer, 1995: 363)*

Mercer builds on Barnes and Todd's exploratory talk definition to develop 'three distinct social modes of thinking'. This term places the social goals of talk firmly at the centre. He warns that these should not be seen as neat descriptive categories; rather, they are analytical categories. However, they provide an interesting overlay to the modes suggested by Phillips and, in particular, Barnes and Todd. He describes *disputational talk*, in which children operate at odds with each other and disagreement features highly. Second, he describes *cumulative talk* in which, although children are positive, they are uncritical of each other's views. Finally he presents his own definition of *exploratory talk*, which refines that suggested by Barnes and Todd into a more sophisticated interaction involving clear, rational and critical discussion. In collaboration with Wegerif and Dawes in 1999, a further refined definition of exploratory talk is described as:

> that in which partners engage critically but constructively with each other's ideas. Statements and suggestions are sought and offered for joint consideration. These may be challenged and counter-challenged, but challenges are justified and alternative hypotheses are offered. In exploratory talk, knowledge is made publicly accountable and reasoning is visible in the talk.
>
> *(Mercer et al., 1999: 97)*

The development of this definition from Mercer's earlier work places more emphasis on accountability, suggesting a higher order of thinking in the development of reasoning. In more recent work, Mercer and Littleton (2007) and Littleton and Mercer (2013) explain the apparent impact of exploratory talk in three ways, suggesting that appropriation, co-construction and transformation all 'link the use of spoken language to the development of reasoning' (2013: 99). Like Phillips, they identify 'markers' or key linguistic features that can be identified as indicators of exploratory talk, for example 'because', 'agree' and 'I think'. The tying of the language mode to specific linguistic indicators sets quite a challenge for talk to be genuinely considered as 'exploratory' as it places an emphasis not only on the positing of hypotheses, provisional meanings or even a trigger of an open dialogic space, but also on a rational and critical mode of thinking indicated by the use of words like 'because' in an expositional function.

Rojas-Drummond et al. (2006) take the modes of talk one step further by suggesting that a 'single over-arching framework' can account for 'productive discussion in education' through the concept of 'co-constructive talk' (2006: 92). In their research, they found that the opportunities for the very specifically defined exploratory talk proposed by Mercer et al. (1999) were task specific, and not necessarily explicit in more open-ended discursive tasks, such as in the discussions of texts. However, there were examples of children adapting their specifically taught exploratory strategies to the task at hand, prompting the researchers to seek a newly defined mode that would encompass this 'joint coordination and collaboration'. They propose a new mode of 'co-constructive talk' which includes 'taking turns, asking for and providing opinions, generating alternatives, reformulating and elaborating on the information being considered, coordinating and negotiating perspectives and seeking agreements' (Rojas-Drummond et al., 2006: 92). It is this framework that suits the task of talking about texts and allows for 'possibility thinking' together because it allows for an open-ended, divergent hypothetical modality, which extends beyond reasoning.

Speech moves and the paradigmatic dimension

As introduced in Chapter 2, Wells (1981) draws attention to the success of communication being a collaborative enterprise, and as such defines two dimensions of dialogue. Along with the 'syntagmatic dimension' or sequential chaining, he highlights the 'paradigmatic dimension', which is what he describes as 'the choice as to what is done at each link in the chain' (1981: 27). These links, which are described by some writers as speech moves (Sinclair and Coulthard, 1975; Wells, 1981; Barnes and Todd, 1995), are a highly pertinent feature of the children's language analyzed in the vignettes. From Wells' perspective they include questions, acceptance, challenges and answers, among many others. Wells argues that the most basic unit of dialogue involves a two-way exchange – 'initiate' and 'respond' – but each response opportunity offers a choice of possible response moves and a number of different frameworks have been developed around this concept. Sinclair and Coulthard (1975: 12) base their categories on the work of Bellack (1966, cited in Sinclair and Coulthard, 1975) and define four basic moves that include a variety of markers: soliciting (questions, commands, requests); responding (reciprocal to soliciting); structuring (setting the context); and reacting (clarifying, synthesizing, expanding). Their categories allow for recognition of the development of ideas, so that reacting and responding are different. Barnes and Todd (1995) identify four main categories of speech move: initiating, eliciting, extending and qualifying, which also expand the basic model and allow for an extended 'chain' of dialogue rather than a two-turn initiation and response. However, in their research they recognize that these moves do not sufficiently identify the cognitive intentions behind the speech move, and that by identifying these strategies, they could be far more specific about the intentions and purpose of the utterances. So, while posited as general move categories, both Sinclair's and Coulthard's, and Barnes' and Todd's classifications are not specific enough to closely analyze how the language might illustrate particular features of thinking.

In a study exploring children's use of 'argumentation stratagems', Anderson et al. (2001: 4) identify a series of stratagems that supported children in the communicative event of 'argument'. They state that: 'We treat reasoning as a process of argumentation. In this view, reasoning inside one's mind consists of a flow of propositions within a discourse of reasoned argument'. Their study was focused on exploring the 'snowballing effect' children using such devices had on their peers. Their list of thirteen different stratagems is useful as a starting point when identifying speech moves, as the research also involved groups of children discussing texts (though in their research the texts were all written). Their stratagems are grouped into six different categories which included gaining the floor, supporting or opposing argument, acknowledging uncertainty, making arguments explicit and using evidence. Particularly useful for this study (and picked up in Chapter 5) is their final category, 'rhetorical extension of the story world', which reflects children's placement of themselves or others into the text scenario.

The 'argumentation' mode bears a close resemblance to the notion of co-constructive or exploratory talk, with one seemingly less prioritized feature. Phillips (1985), Barnes and Todd (1995), Fisher (1993), Mercer et al. (1999) and Rojas-Drummond et al. (2006) all identify the 'hypothetical' as a key element of exploratory or co-constructive modes. Anderson et al. do not incorporate this into their framework of stratagems explicitly, other than to include the 'what if' scenario as a response that takes the reader into the story. Yet to 'suggest or pose' an idea seems a key device to use in a co-constructive reasoning mode and essential in a 'flow of propositions' (Anderson et al., 2001: 4), and could arguably have featured as a category in its own right.

Using co-constructive moves to make meaning from visual texts

Taking the above theories into consideration then, the first focus of attention in this analysis of children's talk is on the function of the 'co-constructive moves'. The term is used to indicate speech moves that illustrate a shift in meaning-making. As such, one turn of speech may actually include more than one co-constructive move, as a speaker takes the meaning-making process forward. In addition to this, the move may not be one of an opposing viewpoint, but may be the extension or rationalization of a possibility; for example, where agreeing with the previous speaker, the new speaker adds a justification or explanation for the first comment. The importance is thus placed on the triggering of response rather than its standpoint. The move of agreeing or supporting a suggestion, or the provision of an answer, suggests a new step in the thinking even if it is one of consolidation.

To generate a coding schedule for the co-constructive dialogue and to illustrate when speech turns were serving a co-constructive purpose, the children's talk in the vignettes was analyzed using a 'constant comparative method' (Glaser and Strauss, 1967). This attempted to strike a balance between approaches where the analysis of dialogue is based on an already devised code, thus limiting the possibilities of new thinking, and those that continually redefine theory, causing coding to become too complex. The approach hits a middle ground by using an iterative process, moving back and forth between what has already been defined and what might need new definition. The data remain central to the process, with the coding and analysis systematically tied to them. The analysis and coding of the children's talk as they discussed different texts led to the identification of nine main moves as integral to the process of co-construction. An extra tenth code was used to categorize moves that related to the process of the interaction, rather than the visual reading of the texts. This focus on the 'interaction frame' of the talk (Barnes and Todd, 1995) is explored in later chapters.

While a basic structure of discourse analysis identifies initiation and response (Wells, 1981), the dialogic functions of the codes in this analysis mean whereas some of them occur only as responses, none of them occur only as initiations as even a question can be used in response to a question. It is the role of these moves within an 'exchange' that is of interest here. Sinclair and Coulthard (1975) identify the move as the smallest 'free' unit (1975: 23) of speech and similarly in Wells' (1999) work on *Dialogic Inquiry*, he defines the smallest unit of meaning in a dialogue the 'move', but argues that it is the 'exchange' into which the move fits that should be the focus for analysis (Wells, 1999: 236). Furthermore, by defining the moves by their relation to each other, the sequence of total turns related to the same initiation can be identified, using Wells' (1981) metaphor of 'chaining'. This also then supports the notion of the opening of a dialogic space of possibility as introduced in Chapter 2, as those moves that afford divergent spaces of possibility can be highlighted. Equally, those moves that convergently propel the sequence of dialogue to a close can also be explored.

When the children's talk was analyzed, there were instances where one complete speech turn – that is, everything said after and before the other speaker's last and next comment – included more than one coded comment, and so both were recorded. This happened where the children responded to the previous speaker then used a further move in the same speech turn as described above. These moves are important as they offer a change of direction for the thinking, and demonstrate intra-mental dialogic processes as well as the inter-mental processes that govern the paradigmatic dimension of the exchanges. That is, they demonstrate how the individual is making meaning independently in addition to the dialogic process. All the comments, or complete phrases deemed a co-constructive move, were therefore assigned a code (see Table 3.1).

TABLE 3.1 The co-constructive moves

Questions Text (QT)	Questions specifically asked about the text to initiate or move the discussion forward
Questions Partner (QP)	Questions specifically asked to find out what a partner is thinking, or to seek clarification about their ideas
Suggests or Poses (SP)	Ideas posited to explain the text, questions or facts, but always containing a suggestion of possibility through words like 'might' or 'maybe'
Uncertainty (U)	Used in instances where the speaker seems unsure, but also where words are used in a non-committal way to 'hedge' or 'repair' the dialogue, or to buy time while formulating a new idea
Extends or Continues (EC)	Where the contribution adds nothing new, but continues an existing idea
Agrees or Supports (AS)	Often just a word that signifies support, but often followed by a question, suggestion or further explanation that is given a different code
Disagrees or Opposes (DO)	These moves are often subtle, for example indicated by ignoring a statement and then suggesting a new idea
Rationalizes or Explains (RE)	A statement that explains an idea, often using 'because' but not always
Statements and Answers (SA)	Moves that appear to finalize a point, offering no suggestion of debate or possibility
Process (P)	These moves are not related to the co-construction of meaning, but are rather about the process of the dialogue itself. They indicate an awareness of the task and its context

To demonstrate the range of co-constructive moves that were found in the children's talk, the first vignette of Harry and Ben (Y1 boys aged six) discussing *The Lady of Shalott* (Waterhouse, 1888) is included in its entirety. The boys were tasked with asking questions about the picture and discussing what it was about. As a result, their discussion includes many exploratory moves as they make suggestions and ask questions of the text. However, other than the initial guidance, they were not directed, and they maintain this exploratory stance throughout all of their discussions. The Lady sits on a boat among reeds in the picture, with a tapestry trailing over the side and candles at one end of the boat.

Demonstrating the codes: Harry and Ben talk about **The Lady of Shalott**

W01[1]	Harry	Right what do you think it is first?
W02	Ben	Well . . . well she's in a boat, cos you can [see the boat] there clearly.
W03	Harry	And what kind . . . And what kind of boat is it? [Is it a motor boat?]

W04	*Ben*	[It's kind of a . . .] or is it a canoeing boat?
W05	*Harry*	Yeah, cos I can't see any oars on it, it must be an engine [boat].
W06	*Ben*	[Or . . .]
W07	*Harry*	It might not be a floating boat.
W08	*Ben*	[Or . . .] yeah that's what's I was just about to say.
W09	*both*	(*both laugh*)
W10	*Ben*	She might just . . . she might just have left it floating, and she'll just sit on there [] having a cup of tea or something.
W11	*Harry*	[And if mmm] . . . and what's all this stuff around it?
W12	*Ben*	Well that . . .
W13	*Harry*	That might be seaweed.
W14	*Ben*	Or . . .
W15	*Harry*	And is it on the river or is on the sea?
W16	*Ben*	(*gestures and nods*) Now that's a good question! Now I don't know that one. No, that's gotta be in a canal innit?
W17	*Harry*	That's got to be in the sea, cos that could be seaweed, couldn't it?
W18	*Ben*	Yeah and then she starts over in that light bit, comes over round here.
W19	*Harry*	Yeah more mmm . . .
W20	*Ben*	She could tie her boat up to that, and then [she] . . .
W21	*Harry*	I know, but, is there any . . . how far does the boat go? Does it end there or does it go right off?
W22	*Ben*	Yeah or it might go off anywhere (*sweeps his arm around*)
W23	*Harry*	Yeah how big is it, and what's all this sticking up?
W24	*Ben*	Might be plants, might be seaweed . . .
W25	*Harry*	Yeah I think it's probably seaweed that's the most likeliest thing. And are there any fish in there?
W26	*Ben*	[Or] . . . fish in there?
W27	*Harry*	(*laughs*)
W28	*Ben*	There might be goldfish?
W29	*Harry*	Might be goldfish, might be sharks? (*Ben mishears him and thinks he has said 'sock'*)
W30	*Ben*	Might be 'socks' . . . (*looks confused*) What?
W31	*Harry*	And what's all this thing? Well that . . .
W32	*Ben*	Well they might be like goldfish, like.
W33	*Harry*	They might be other kinds of fish. They might be haddock.
W34	*Ben*	Mmm
W35	*Harry*	Or it might be . . . mmm any other of fish? Might be skate or it might be a cat . . . cat fish . . . ?
W36	*Ben*	You mean cat fish?
W37	*Harry*	Yeah . . . Or it might be a cat that's dived in to catch the fish there and [then it kinds like] . . .
W38	*Ben*	That's the fish . . . and this kind of silvery black bit is the cat.
W39	*Harry*	Yeah and it's trying to catch it and this lady's gone out to catch the cat and then so she can catch the fish.
W40	*Ben*	Right, umm . . .

W41   *Harry*   And then the fish gets eaten by the lady.
W42   *Ben*   Yeah.
W43   *Harry*   Yeah that would be kind of wouldn't it? That would fit. I'm quite good at doing all these because, umm, I'm in a school that goes around solving mysteries. It's called the Pig Snout.

Harry and Ben's discussion serves as a sound starting point for coding, as there are examples of all of the codes identified within the short discussion, as follows.

QT-Questions Text

This is a question about something in the text. It is classified as a co-constructive move as it is an initiation in identifying the problem to be solved. The language markers 'what', 'where', 'why', 'how' and 'are' denote this move. Ambiguities sometimes arise where the question is directed to the other child, for example to clarify what they have said. In that case the code would not be QT but QP (Questions Partner) as the clarification relates to the process of dialogue, not the co-construction of meaning. The very first question in the vignette is coded as (QP) as it is asking for the opinion of Ben, to kick-start the discussion. However, later on Harry asks:

W11   *Harry*   [And if mmm] . . . and what's all this stuff around it?
W12   *Ben*   Well that . . .
W13   *Harry*   That might be seaweed.

While the question is directed to Ben, it is directly about a feature of the text. In fact, Harry does not give Ben a chance to answer as he makes a suggestion himself.

This code denotes the second highest frequency of comment within the discussions by Harry and Ben, and is not surprising, given that the only prompt the children had to talk about the text was to ask questions about it, to 'discuss what it is all about'. The frequency of the code is a reminder that this is a discussion taking place in a classroom context, and the children are completing a task. However, the co-constructive move is used exclusively by Harry and can be seen as an indicator of him taking charge of the discussion. Notwithstanding this, the move does serve to open a dialogue about the text, and to move it on when ideas have been exhausted. Over the two vignettes there are twelve moves coded with QT and all of them are assigned to Harry.

QP-Questions Partner

As suggested above, the code QP is more likely to be assigned to moves that ask for clarity or the expansion of ideas. It could therefore also be used in response to another question. The difference between this code and the previous one is that it is an indicator of process and fits more neatly into Barnes' and Todd's (1995) 'interaction frame' category. These moves still move the dialogue along, but they are concentrated on the process of meaning-making rather than the content of ideas. When the children ask each other, for example, 'What's that?', the question is directed at the text, not the partner, so would be given the QT–Questions Text code. However, when they ask each other specifically about their thinking or intended meaning, then the QP–Questions Partner code is used. For example:

W33	Harry	They might be other kinds of fish. They might be haddock.
W34	Ben	Mmm
W35	Harry	Or it might be . . . mmm any other of fish? Might be skate or it might be a cat . . . cat fish . . . ?
W36	Ben	You mean cat fish?
W37	Harry	Yeah . . . Or it might be a cat that's dived in to catch the fish there and [then it kinds like] . . .

In this sequence the children are discussing the possible types of fish that may be in the water surrounding the Lady of Shalott's boat. Harry is checking Ben's intended meaning by asking him to clarify, and possibly by offering an alternative (not catfish, but a cat) the response takes a creative turn (it could be a cat, cats like fish . . .).

SP-Suggests or Poses

This code is used for instances where one child puts forward an idea to explain the text. They may be questions, but not always. The discriminating factor is the use of a word or phrase that signifies 'possibility' rather than 'fact'. The language used suggests that the comment is debatable, and may include a phrase such as 'doesn't it?' In this sequence Ben's comment is assigned the SP-Suggests or Poses code. However, Harry's second comment is not, as although it contains an element of possibility, shown by the use of the word 'probably', it is a continuation of the first idea.

W23	Harry	Yeah how big is it, and what's all this sticking up?
W24	Ben	Might be plants, might be seaweed . . .
W25	Harry	Yeah I think it's probably seaweed that's the most likeliest thing. And are there any fish in there?

This code appears with the highest frequency across both of Harry and Ben's discussions, suggesting that the children are motivated to discuss and agree, rather than just make statements. The use of the move is fairly evenly spread between the two boys, with a pattern of Ben using this move more frequently towards the end of the discussions. There is an element of social awareness connected to comments of this kind as they imply a goal of negotiation and collaboration, rather than statement of fact. The code rarely features as an initiation comment in Harry and Ben's discussion, and occurs more often in response to QT–Questions Text. The typical specific markers that indicate its use are 'might', 'isn't it' and other provisional or hypothetical language.

AS-Agrees or Supports

The code AS-Agrees or Supports is used when a comment is a positive response to the previous comment, but serves no other dialogic purpose. In saying 'yeah', the ideas of the previous speaker are supported. If the previous speaker's phrase is repeated with nothing added, the code AS is given. Across the two vignettes, it is Ben who uses this move most frequently, and this is not surprising given the number of questions asked by Harry. Like SP-Suggests or Poses, the balance of the use of this move becomes more evenly spread as the discussion progresses between the two boys. On its own, this comment does not invite further response.

W41   *Harry*   And then the fish gets eaten by the lady.
W42   *Ben*   Yeah.

However, if the speaker then continues to say something else, this is then coded individually. For example:

W36   *Ben*   You mean cat fish?
W37   *Harry*   Yeah . . . Or it might be a cat that's dived in to catch the fish there and [then it kinds like] . . .

In this second sequence Harry is developing his own idea, but he starts the turn by agreeing with Ben before extending his ideas.

EC-Extends or Continues

If the speaker takes the idea forward and adds to it, this is given the code EC-Extends or Continues. This code is not an initiating code as it shows a response to an idea. It may mean that the idea has not developed, and is just a continuation of a theme. The children often list a series of possibilities, following on from each other. In discussion about the Waterhouse painting, they list different types of fish, extending the same idea and ultimately creating a narrative to continue the idea further. The comments highlighted below are coded EC-Extends or Continues:

W32   *Ben*   Well they might be like goldfish, like.
W33   *Harry*   They might be other kinds of fish. They might be haddock.
W34   *Ben*   Mmm
W35   *Harry*   Or it might be . . . mmm any other of fish? Might be skate or it might be a cat . . . cat fish . . . ?

There is a high frequency of EC-Extends or Continues comments, demonstrating that the children are listening to each other and adding to the idea expressed. However, these comments are often lists, for example this list of fish and the earlier list of boats. The code is not used for comments that generate a new idea, but rather for a continuation of a theme, and the comments are largely uncritical of the previous suggestion, aligning with Mercer's definition of 'cumulative talk' (1995, 1996).

RE-Rationalizes or Explains

This is also a response code and linked to EC-Extends or Continues. The inclusion of 'because' (or abbreviations of this) will typify these statements and they often involve the creation of a narrative reason for an event, though this is not always the case, as the causality may be more implied than stated. The inclusion of 'because' would define this as Mercer et al.'s (1999) definition of 'exploratory talk'. This code may follow AS-Agrees or Supports or DO-Disagrees or Opposes, or explain the ideas suggested by the previous speaker without overtly agreeing with them. A typical sequence that features this co-constructive move is:

W03	Harry	And what kind . . . And what kind of boat is it? [Is it a motor boat?]
W04	Ben	[It's kind of a . . .] or is it a canoeing boat?
W05	Harry	Yeah, cos I can't see any oars on it, it must be an engine [boat].

In the sequence above, the children are discussing the type of boat in which the Lady of Shalott is sitting. Harry seems to agree (by saying 'yeah') then disagrees with Ben's idea that it could be a canoe, by rationalizing that because he can't see any oars, the boat must have an engine. The children are equal in their use of rationalizing explanatory moves.

DO-Disagrees or Opposes

Like AS-Agrees or Supports, this code only occurs in response to a comment, never as an initiating statement. This code is evident when the speaker rejects a previous statement, not always by openly disagreeing, for example by saying 'I don't think that is right', but also when a subtler rejection has been used, for example ignoring the previous idea and offering a new view, as Harry does above. In the turns below, Harry rejects Ben's suggestion about the waterway being a canal and suggests an alternative, supporting his idea by offering an explanation about seaweed:

| W16 | Ben | (*gestures and nods*) Now that's a good question! Now I don't know that one. No, that's gotta be in a canal innit? |
| W17 | Harry | That's got to be in the sea, cos that could be seaweed, couldn't it? |

As a co-constructive move, this code occurs less than any other across the two discussions, only twice in fact, and both times is made by Harry (not surprising given the amount of agreement that Ben offers), which may further suggest an underlying goal that the children have of maintaining some social cohesion, as they are cautious to explicitly disagree with a previous suggestion.

SA-Statements or Answers

This is a more definite opinion than SP-Suggests or Poses: 'it is' or 'that is' rather than 'it might be'. It may occur in response to a question or suggestion, or as an isolated occurrence. The two have been separated as there is an element of flexibility in SP-Suggests or Poses that is not evident in SA-Statements and Answers. This code is used not only for initiations, but also for responses if a statement answer has been given. It would seem to imply that there is not much more to say on the particular issue as it leaves no space for dispute. This suggests that even if used as an initial comment, it is quite a closed comment, leaving the dialogue with nowhere to go unless the ideas are disputed.

| W24 | *Ben* | Might be plants, might be seaweed . . . |
| W25 | *Harry* | Yeah I think it's probably seaweed that's the most likeliest thing. And are there any fish in there? |

With this turn, Harry repeats Ben's suggestion that there is seaweed – and reinforces it. He then moves on to a new idea (about fish), effectively finishing the seaweed discussion. Like DO-Disagrees or Opposes, this co-constructive move does not occur frequently through the transcripts, reinforcing the suggestion that the children are keen to engage in a discussion, not just 'answer the question'.

U-Uncertainty

Sometimes speakers are explicit in their uncertainty, for example 'I don't know'. However, this code is also used when speakers leave comments unfinished or use a comment such as 'maybe . . . ' to respond vaguely without either agreeing or disagreeing. In his research, Fairclough (1992) coined the phrase 'hedging' (1992: 116) to describe language that offers a tone of provisionality, or makes the language used less extreme, and this can usefully be adopted here. The term is adapted to include a type of non-committal response that enables the turn of speech to move to the other speaker, rather than places where a speaker seems about to suggest something and is cut off by the other person. In these cases a degree of caution was needed to make sure that meaning was not imposed on the talk in the process of interpretation, a warning given by Edwards and Westgate (1987) in their review of research about classroom talk. For this, the original video data offered a richer representation of the event from which to interpret meaning.

W39	*Harry*	Yeah and it's trying to catch it and this lady's gone out to catch the cat and then so she can catch the fish.
W40	*Ben*	Right, umm . . .
W41	*Harry*	And then the fish gets eaten by the lady.

In this response to Harry's suggestion, Ben seems reluctant to suggest anything for definite, but he does not dismiss the idea; this allows Harry the time to continue with his creative story about why there might be a cat in the picture.

P-Process

The final code sits slightly to the side of the other moves and is not linked to para-digmatic chaining or in Barnes' and Todd's definition the 'content frame' (1995: 145). Rather, it is a comment that demonstrates that the speaker is aware of the process they are engaged in. That is, they are trying to make sense of text as a task for a teacher. Barnes and Todd refer to this as the 'interaction frame'. As such, the comments that are coded P-Process exist as reflections on the process, as 'asides', if a performance analogy is followed. An awareness of one's own thinking and progress is deemed an important part of both critical and creative thinking (see Chapter 5) and can still be classified as a co-constructive move, as it suggests the notion of more than one 'voice': the internal onlooker, reviewing the progress of the thinking and the dialogue. Occasionally the children look at the camera, showing their awareness of the co-constructive situation they are in, and this is recorded in the transcript. However, this code is assigned only to actual speech that demonstrates the children thinking about the process, not just being aware of it. Neither is it assigned to joint laughter at a shared joke. In many ways the move seems to demonstrate a sophisticated approach to the discussion as the children are simultaneously aware of the speech event as an educational task, sometimes with value judgements about their success in achieving it. This is particularly apparent in Harry's comments, for example:

W43   *Harry*   Yeah that would be kind of wouldn't it? That would fit. I'm quite good at doing all these because, umm, I'm in a school that goes around solving mysteries. It's called the Pig Snout.

A closer analysis of this code across the different vignettes occurs in Chapter 6 which looks in detail at the importance of reflection in and on the process of co-construction. While the comments that indicate this stance are not frequent within the children's talk, they do demonstrate a 'framing' of the dialogue and a control of the task at hand by the children.

Building a model of co-constructive talk

From the initial description of the coded moves above, it can be reasonably argued that Harry and Ben's discussions fall within the 'over-arching' framework of co-constructive talk proposed by Rojas-Drummond et al. (2006). The moves that have been coded propel this co-construction forward, and while the systematic achievement of a shared understanding may not always be apparent, the overall joint construction of meaning is evidenced in the moves the children use. Having established this, and having systematically coded the co-constructive moves the children use, the ways that these moves work together can now be explored in detail. This time, the discussion that Harry and Ben have about the René Magritte picture *Golconde* (1953) is used to demonstrate the functions of the co-constructive moves. The picture shows a multitude of figures wearing long coats and bowler hats, suspended in mid-air in front of and above buildings.

Demonstrating the functions of the co-constructive moves: Harry and Ben talk about Golconde

M01	*Ben*	A kind of a film.
M02	*Harry*	Yeah, what film is it from? And are these people here, (*points*) are these men or ladies?
M03	*Ben*	Men. (*Both pause to look*) . . . They might be . . . (*looks at camera*)
M04	*Harry*	And . . . But are they womens? They might be black raindrops that look like womens, mightn't they?
M05	*Ben*	They . . . .
M06	*Harry*	And are these houses or hotels or flats . . . that are there?
M07	*Ben*	[Maybe]
M08	*Harry*	Because it must be . . .
M09	*Ben*	[Hmm] no they're hotels . . .
M10	*Harry*	They're hotels? What makes you thinks they are hotels?
M11	*Ben*	Because some people have stopped to go . . .
M12	*Harry*	Yes. There's a door leading into it.
M13	*Ben*	Well, the door . . . cos they're big, the door might go down there, down there, down to the bottom.
M14	*Harry*	But . . . I wonder if they are going up or down. That's a question isn't it?
M15	*Ben*	[Hmm].
M16	*Harry*	Because they're going down on . . . They look like . . .
M17	*Ben*	[Cos cos they're on the floor.]
M18	*Harry*	I know, but they might have been taking off . . . and how are they getting up there?
M19	*Ben*	[Yeah . . . or . . .] . . . or they might have jumped out of a helicopter.
M20	*Harry*	I know. How can an aeroplane or a helicopter hold so many people in it?
M21	*Ben*	Well, there could be one, one, one, one (*gestures*) . . . it could be like . . .
M22	*Harry*	[There could be ten of them]
M23	*Ben*	And then they'd set out of another ten . . . and . . . another ten and another ten and another ten.
M24	*Harry*	[And] then they might all fly back up again and they might go and land somewhere else, mighten they?
M25	*Ben*	Yeah . . . and do something . . .
M26	*Harry*	I think that's about it we can think of!
M27	*Ben*	(*looks at camera*)

The moves that feature in the co-construction of meaning can be further organized by their predominant function within a dialogue, which leads to a discussion of the 'pattern' of moves within the vignettes. They can be categorized into three inter-linking phases. Initially, though these may occur at different points within the dialogue, there are those moves that indicate an opening of the dialogic space of possibility. At this point suggestions that may be put forward as hypotheses or

potential meaning (SP-Suggests or Poses) are provisional and offered for negotiation. Within this divergent phase there are questions that are about the text
itself, where the participants 'wonder' about it (QT-Questions Text). Although
these may appear to be directed at another party, they are about the text, not the
respondent, and offer possibility and potentiality. These moves are creative thinking moves, divergent in nature, and inviting conjecture. Ultimately, they may have
the goal of solution-finding, but they are initiations and open up possibility. They
are the triggers for 'possibility thinking' (Craft, 2000) and are not geared towards
critical thinking or convergent solutions, but towards divergence and creative solutions. They can be called *divergent moves*. In Harry and Ben's discussion about
Golconde, they suddenly hit on the idea that the figures might be rising, not falling:

M14   Harry   But . . . I wonder if they are going up or down. That's a question
                isn't it?

This idea hooks both children's imaginations and they work together to initiate a
series of suggestions and questions that allow for creative responses and further possibility thinking. Even their rationalizations and explanations provide a springboard
for further thinking:

M18   Harry   I know, but they might have been taking off . . . and how are they
                getting up there?
M19   Ben   [Yeah . . . or . . .] . . . or they might have jumped out of a
                helicopter.
M20   Harry   I know. How can an aeroplane or a helicopter hold so many peo-
                ple in it?
M21   Ben   Well, there could be one, one, one, one (*gestures*) . . . it could be
                like . . .
M22   Harry   [There could be ten of them]
M23   Ben   And then they'd set out of another ten . . . and . . . another ten
                and another ten and another ten.
M24   Harry   [And] then they might all fly back up again and they might go and
                land somewhere else, mighten they?

The second inter-linking phase of dialogue occurs within the exploratory space of
dialogue and understanding or dialogic space of possibility. This extends the theory
of Wegerif (2008a, 2008b) who discusses the space between speakers of construction and reconstruction, by suggesting that there are specific co-constructive moves,
and then linguistic markers that denote them, which enable the maintenance of this
space. While the thinking remains in the space, the meanings are provisional, as
discussed by both Lyle (1993) and Maybin (1994) and explored earlier in Chapter
2. This then is the mid-point between problem-finding and solution-finding, and
at this point there are many possible or potential meanings. The space can be *wid-
ened* through engaging with additional similar ideas. The tendency of Harry and

Ben to create lists, of fish types in the Waterhouse discussion or buildings, can be seen as a widening of the space, as more and more possibilities are explored.

The space can also be *deepened*, through focusing on the detail of one idea and exploring every angle related to it, as in the sequence above explaining about the number of helicopters needed to carry so many people. This phase is indicated by comments where participants extend or continue the ideas as responses (EC-Extends or Continues). It may also be indicated by a respondent showing signs of uncertainty about a previous comment (U-Uncertainty). This is the space of possibility and uncertainty, and it could be argued that while it might seem uncomfortable, as no solutions or definitions have yet been agreed, it is an important space in which to feel secure. This extends the search for meaning rather than too quickly finding a solution. In a connection also explored more recently by Wegerif (2008a), this brings to mind the literary concept of 'negative capability', first espoused by Keats in 1817 (in Keats et al. 2002), in a letter in which he recounted an enjoyable discussion he had been having with friends. In the letter he describes negative capability as ' . . . when man is capable of being in uncertainties, Mysteries, doubts without any irritable reaching after fact and reason' (2002: 41–42). This pleasure in engaging in talk and thought needs no resolution, as the joy is in occupying the dialogic space. It can be argued that this poetic stance, the occupancy of this dialogic space without ever moving to converge, might lead to disjointed and unresolved problems. However, in the vignettes of Harry and Ben, this stance allows them to explore possibility without being hindered by the need for correct answers.

The final inter-linking phase of dialogue is one in which the thinking begins to converge towards a satisfactory (for the participants at least) resolution. The speech markers that indicate this dimension of thinking and comprehension may be responses to suggestions or questions that offer no further link and appear definitive. This can be equally true of agreement (AS-Agrees or Supports) or disagreement (DO-Disagrees or Opposes). Sometimes the opening comment might offer no space for possibility, as indicated by a statement or answer (SA-Statements and Answers). More extended responses may still be classified as convergent thinking as they may indicate reasoning or the rationalization behind a hypothesis (RE-Reasons or Explains). This shows a high level of critical thinking, moving towards meaning-making, and these moves can be described as *convergent moves*. This does not mean that the dialogue will not move back into a more fluid and less defined state, as the direction the dialogue takes is controlled by the next speaker, not the previous one. For Harry and Ben, when discussing Magritte, they are both satisfied by their solution about helicopters, so much so that Harry marks the end of the discussion explicitly: 'That's about it we can think of!', he declares. This model of co-constructive talk can be illustrated as a diagram, to provide a visual landscape against which to map the discourse of the meaning-making event and further to understand the function of the co-constructive moves within it (Figure 3.1).

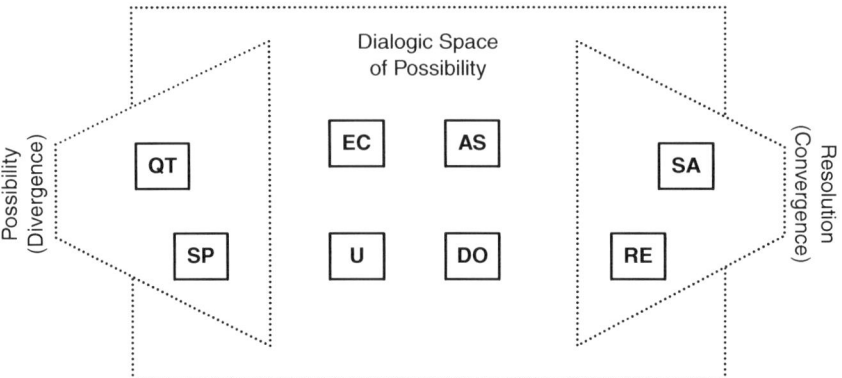

FIGURE 3.1 A model of co-constructive talk

The coding of the co-constructive moves is useful because it tells us something about the patterns of language the children use. It highlights just how prevalent are moves that have a hypothetical flavour in these young children's language, and this makes sense in light of the task they were given. The sophistication with which the children handle the discussions is explored in more detail in Chapter 7, but suffice to say that running parallel to meaning–making is the negotiation of co-construction, and this requires a particular approach to managing the dialogue that even young children seem able to take if engaged in talk in an environment that is supportive in promoting talk.

Dialogic chains of thinking

While the dialogic space of possibility exists because of a continual fluid motion of provisional ideas communicated through signifiers of meaning, there are particular response possibilities or language markers (Phillips, 1985) that open up this space, and invite a divergence of possibilities. To accept or promote meaning as provisional, the speaker must indicate this through the phrasing of their ideas. This can be achieved very simply by intonation (a rising inflection) or by the use of questions such as 'isn't it?' or 'doesn't it?' This shows not only that affirmation is sought, but also indicates that the speaker accepts that their meaning is provisional and open to change. This style of dialogue is particularly relevant in a co-construction of meaning event, where the goal of the dialogue is to find a solution or an agreed meaning.

However, the research of Barnes and Todd (1995) suggests that the sequence of ideas in a dialogue is even more complex than this. They found that often utterances carried meanings across long sequences of dialogue, and that these were not easily isolated into one category of meaning but found in cycles. This idea originates in the work of Sinclair and Coulthard (1975), who describe sequences of dialogue as 'cycles' (1975: 12). This implies a more complex interpretation of dialogues than simply a speaker/response relationship. The speaker may be picking up themes and developing ideas from more than the previous comment, and may be drawing on the development of their own hypothesis without much attention to the other participant. Tannen (1989) indicates that: 'conversation is not a matter of two (or more) people alternatively taking the role of speaker and listener, but rather that both speaking and listening include elements and traces of the other' (1989: 12). The roles are therefore not strictly divided into neat turns, but are rather cycles of meaning, and threads of understanding dynamically weave their way through the dialogue. This makes the concept of a dialogic space of possibility even more important as it provides a 'virtual' holding place for all ideas, both within current use (that is, within a particular sequence of dialogue) and also as an access to past ideas and experiences. Within this space occur chains of dialogue (following Wells' 1981 description of the paradigmatic dimension) where an initial comment provokes a series of responses attuned to the same idea. This is, of course, complex, as Barnes and Todd suggest above (1995: 140), where meanings evolve over several exchanges; yet mapping these chains enables an analysis of the inter-thinking that the children are engaged in and the features of their responses to the texts.

The model of co-constructive talk suggests a movement from divergent to convergent moves. But this is a model and real dialogue does not necessarily follow the same pattern of movement. Sequences of connected exchanges can be analyzed by linking moves that stem from the same initiation. These dialogic chains of thinking show the total number of exchanges related to one idea. In Harry and Ben's discussion of the Magritte picture, there are three such chains. Within these sequences, the opening divergent moves are often initiated by the use of connectives ('and' or 'but') which the children may use to link to the previous comment. However, analyzed closely, it can be seen that often the children precede their comments with the use of a connective word or phrase when the comment is essentially a new dialogic chain of thinking. The overall dialogue relates to the speech event of making meaning from the picture, otherwise the connective does not represent a continuation of thinking.

The three chains increase in length, moving from six to nine then sixteen turns before stopping abruptly: 'I think that's about it we can think of!', declares Harry as the final convergent statement. Mapping the dialogue in this way demonstrates how the children appear not to seek definite resolution; they are happy just to explore ideas with negative capability. This can be seen in the second chain below where Harry initiates the chain by asking a question, and it finishes with Ben continuing an idea about the door before making a new suggestion. Harry's next turn (M14) initiates a new chain, and he ignores Ben's suggestion:

M06	*Harry*	And are these houses or hotels or flats . . . that are there?
M07	*Ben*	[maybe]
M08	*Harry*	Because it must be . . .
M09	*Ben*	[hmm] no they're hotels . . .

M10	*Harry*	They're hotels? What makes you thinks they are hotels?
M11	*Ben*	Because some people have stopped to go . . .
M12	*Harry*	Yes . . . There's a door leading into it
M13	*Ben*	Well, the door . . . cos they're big, the door might go down there, down there, down to the bottom
M14	*Harry*	But . . . I wonder if they are going up or down. That's a question isn't it?

The mapping demonstrates how chains are continued beyond the defined convergent point of the dialogue. In the opening exchange, Ben begins with a statement, a seemingly convergent point, offering little potential for the idea to continue:

| *M01* | *Ben* | A kind of a film |
| *M02* | *Harry* | Yeah, What film is it from? And are these people here, *(points)* are these men or ladies? |

In what appears to be quite a sophisticated move by Harry, he acknowledges the previous statement, questions it and puts forward a new question. This is perhaps the point to remember that these children are in Year 1, and by no means defined by their teacher as being outstanding in their ability to communicate, yet their dialogue is complex and sophisticated, as they engage with the goal of co-construction. Analyzing the dialogue through looking at the chains enables us to see how the children use co-constructive moves to develop their thinking, and how their dialogue ebbs and flows as ideas take form and are either developed or discarded by the respondent. As the discussion progresses, the ideas become more fluid, evidenced by the number of turns in which they acknowledge the preceding comment (usually by agreement) and then take the thinking further, not just by extending and continuing the idea, but also by suggesting and posing new ideas. This is true for all of the discussions that Harry and Ben have, with their ideas extending into longer dialogic chains of thinking as their discussions progress.

For Harry and Ben, the QT–Questions Text coded comments tend to be situated at the start of the sequences, demonstrating a divergent, enquiry-led approach to making meaning. However, the chains of thinking do not always end with a clear statement or explanation to 'conclude' the idea, suggesting that either the children are content to leave the problem unresolved by offering a metaphorical ellipsis (the delight of negative capability) or as far as they are concerned they have fulfilled the task. Alternatively, the sequences can be seen to suggest that with little encouragement the children are happy to engage in co-constructive debate, without apparently feeling frustrated or uncomfortable with the lack of a resolution or defined answer.

Chapter summary

The chapter began by exploring theories of different modes of talk evident in classrooms. Although the moves identified by Sinclair and Coulthard (1975), Wells

(1981), Barnes and Todd (1995) and Anderson et al. (2001) are useful pointers, it is important that the analysis of the co-constructive dialogue allows for an identification of moves that may not have been previously recognized, and are specific to this particular communicative situation, children reading and talking about visual texts. Ten codes were used to analyze the children's talk (exemplified by Harry and Ben), drawing on these existing frames where appropriate. However, rather than tying moves to specific linguistic markers (even if there are common words and phrases used that tend to indicate particular moves), the *function* of each co-constructive move was the focus, and from this a model of co-constructive dialogue was formed. The two frames of analysis, 'content' and 'interaction', suggested by Barnes and Todd (1995) are useful ways of differentiating between language that relates to the process of the social interaction and the task itself, and language that directly leads to the co-construction of meaning. In this chapter, the content frame was in the spotlight and formed the basis of the model.

The model emphasizes the importance of the functions of the co-constructive moves and the purpose they serve in propelling the dialogue forward. Using Harry and Ben's discussion, the notion of dialogic chains of thinking was explored, highlighting the movement of ideas between the two speakers. The next chapter will look at the other side of the dialogue coin, focusing on the ideas that the children have and how their critical and creative thinking is co-constructed as they make sense of text. It examines some of the language markers that indicate that this is happening, though is careful not to assume that similar markers have the same co-constructive function.

Note

1 As two vignettes of Harry and Ben are explored, they are differentiated by the line turns for clarity. In the discussion about the Waterhouse painting, each line number is preceded by W. In the Magritte discussion, each line number is preceded by M.

4

THINKING TOGETHER

Responding critically and creatively

So far we have concentrated on the linguistic properties of children's language as they talk together to make meaning from text. However, now our attention turns to the thinking that their language indicates, to consider how children can think critically and creatively together as they make meaning. Littleton and Mercer (2013) describe 'inter-thinking' as the co-construction of meaning or inter-subjectivity, but other writers have considered the differing qualities of thinking from an intra-mental perspective and there has been much debate about the nature of critical and creative thinking, considering how these might be different and whether it is useful to define them separately. Moseley et al. argue that there is little point in doing so, as they overlap in so many situations and can rather be seen as interdependent (Moseley et al., 2005: 119). Yet the nature of that interdependence does need exploring, and so critical and creative thinking can be seen as different modes of thought, or to link to different co-constructive moves in a dialogue.

This is particularly true if we consider the terms 'divergent' and 'convergent' as relating to creative and critical thinking. The definition of these 'frames of mind' originates in the work of Hudson (1968) who broadly linked them as inclinations towards logical and scientific subjects (convergent), or creative art areas (divergent). While his terms were rigid and defined characteristics of people, or rather 'clever schoolboys' (1968: 1), the terms can be usefully adopted to describe modes of *thinking* rather than types of *thinkers*. The skills associated with critical thinking can be described as more convergent, leading to solution; for example, reasoning, clarifying, analyzing and rationalizing – in other words, *solution-finding*. In fact, the term 'skills' is itself debatable as many writers include the term 'disposition' to highlight an attitude towards thinking, as opposed to a skill that may or may not be used. As Claxton (2007) argues, the difference can be highlighted as between ability and being disposed to use that ability (2007: 119).

While critical thinking is more convergently focused on solution-finding, creative thinking can be described as a divergent process, for example imagining or making connections, which Craft (2000) describes as 'possibility thinking', aspects of which include 'being imaginative, asking questions and playing' (2000: 1). Creative thinking can, then, be seen as *problem-finding*, or for Nickerson, 'a special kind of problem-solving' (Nickerson, 1999: 394). Effective problem-solvers are sometimes described as being able to 'think outside the box', valuing their creative and divergent approaches and recognizing their disposition to not be satisfied with one way of thinking, and not taking Paul's 'monological' stance (1987, as discussed in Chapter 2). For Burnard et al. (2006), possibility thinking has questioning at the core, with a central feature of 'pondering and positing "what if" scenarios in the mind' (2006: 255). It is this hypothesizing that enables the opening of a dialogic space, where all is possible and ideas are not bound. The disadvantage of starting with the premise that critical and creative thinking involve seemingly opposing characteristics is that this could be viewed as over-simplification, a neat pigeon-holing of complex cognitive processes. For example, in defining the 'independent dimensions', Nickerson states,

> Creative thinking is expansive, innovative, inventive, unconstrained thinking. It is associated with exploration and idea generation. It is daring, uninhibited, fanciful, imaginative, free-spirited, unpredictable, revolutionary. Critical thinking is focused, disciplined, logical, constrained thinking. It is down to earth, realistic, practical, staid, dependable, conservative.
>
> *(Nickerson, 1999: 397)*

But he goes on to argue that if they are viewed as polar opposites, the implication is created that, for example, more creative thinking means less critical thinking. In fact, Nickerson argues that critical and creative thinking are two sides of the same coin. This suggests that while it does make sense to separate the two, their interdependence must be recognized, as well as the apparent dichotomy that occurs when thinking is simultaneously divergent and convergent.

The terms 'divergent thinking' and 'convergent thinking' are useful as they have the dialogic associations described in the previous chapter. Divergent thinking suggests the concept of dialogically opening an idea by posing a possibility, whereas convergent thinking suggests resolving or closing an issue, by offering, for example, an explanation that seems to offer no further possibility. This may be done with another thinker, or alone, by taking a dialogical stance (Paul, 1987). In language, following this suggestion of 'opening' or 'closing down' an idea, divergent co-constructive moves are those that open up a dialogic space of possibility between speakers, while convergent thinking moves lead to a conclusion. This should not be taken to suggest that convergent thinking moves are detrimental to a discussion, as they are absolutely necessary if an appropriate solution is to be found. Keats et al.'s (2002) space of 'negative capability' may be convenient for poets, but does not lead to decision or product. Equally, from a normative perspective, a narrow, single-minded, or even monological approach might not find the best solution. Clearly, there is a balance within the dialogic space of possibility, and ideally a fluid movement between both divergent and convergent thinking, to provide an opportunity for both exploratory ideas and a move to a critical solution. In the discussions that Harry and Ben have, they do not always end their chains of thinking with convergent co-constructive moves; equally, in the other vignettes the children do not always start their chains of thinking with questions or suggestions. The impact of those approaches will be explored later in the chapter. Initially, however, our attention turns to specific linguistic markers that might suggest possibility thinking and exploratory talk are happening, though remaining cautious not to assume that because a marker is present it is consistent in its function.

Critical and creative language

Mercer's work detailing 'I think . . . because' as an indicator of exploratory talk is well known, but it is worth considering how subtle language choices can support the co-construction and maintenance of the dialogue. As suggested, the patterns of language that are apparent in the children's talk show a prevalence of hypothetical linguistic markers that enable a provisionality of meaning and, therefore, the possibility or potential of additional ideas and creative thinking. These language markers include words and phrases such as 'might be', 'maybe' and 'I wonder if'. They can be termed 'potentiating' or 'possibility markers' rather than 'hypothetical' as while they create a potential space for the exploration of ideas, they may not constitute a definite hypothesis or the set promotion of a theory.

The children use particular words, phrases and repetitions in their dialogue as a means of interweaving the creation of meaning and maintaining a social harmony between themselves (to be explored in Chapter 7). The analysis of each individual vignette demonstrates that these patterns are particular to each individual case, as the children respond to each other and pick up their language patterns in addition to creating their own. This can also be exemplified through the dialogue between Hannah and Anna, two Y1 children who also talk about *The Lady of Shalott*. Their whole discussion is included here so that later, extracts can be used and understood within the context of the whole. In their discussion the children particularly use 'I wonder . . . ?', 'probably' and 'maybe' to explore possible ideas, but also to move their dialogue forward:

01	*Hannah*	I think she's just <u>probably</u> sitting on a boat on . . . water?
02	*Anna*	I think she kinda wants to see like loads of pretty things, isn't she?
03	*Hannah*	While she's sailing on the boat . . . Why's her skirt hanging out in the water?
04	*Anna*	I don't know, <u>probably</u> she just wants to get her skirt wet so she can dry it, so, cos she, look it's quite muddy isn't it? (*Points at screen*)
05	*Hannah*	Mm

06	*Anna*	It's quite muddy.
07	*Hannah*	<u>Maybe</u> it's muddy cos she [went] . . .
08	*Anna*	[Went] in the mud.
09	*Hannah*	Yeah then she needs like, like went on the boat and she like hanged it [over in the water] . . .
10	*Anna*	[Yeah, so, what]
11	*Hannah*	. . . to clean it all up.
12	*Anna*	Um <u>I wonder</u> why her hair's so long. <u>Maybe</u> she's never ever cut it.
13	*Hannah*	<u>Maybe</u> it could just like grows (*holds hair*).
14	*Anna*	<u>I wonder</u> why she's got that black thing on her.
15	*Hannah*	It's <u>probably</u> like a little belt to keep her skirt up so it doesn't fall down (*gestures*).
16	*Anna*	Yeah <u>I wonder</u> why she needs to clean her dress, cos . . .
17	*Hannah*	<u>Maybe</u> she like fell over in the mud cos she probably tripped over a stone or a [ ] and she . . . flat into the mud (*gestures*).
18	*Anna*	She could put it in a dishwasher couldn't she?
19	*Hannah*	(*Laughs*) . . . Dishwasher?!
20	*Anna*	(*Laughs*) No I mean a . . . thingy!

[long pause]

21	*Anna*	<u>I wonder</u> what those white things are (*points*).
22	*Hannah*	They look like candles to me . . . If you look closer you can <u>probably</u> see it.
23	*Anna*	<u>Probably</u>, I think it's probably night time.
24	*Hannah*	That's why she's got candles on the boat . . . It's dark sort of around there isn' it?
25	*Anna*	Yeah.
26	*Hannah*	If you go right back you can actually see if it's really dark (*leans back in chair*).
27	*Anna*	Um, it's kind of, I think she's not allowed in the house cos she's so muddy . . .
28	*Hannah*	Yeah, so she had to go and wash herself.
29	*Anna*	. . . and she has to have tea on the boat.
30	*Hannah*	Tea on the boat! (*laughs*)
31	*Anna*	Um, <u>I wonder</u> what . . . um . . . <u>I wonder</u> why she's got a big boat not a little rowing boat.
32	*Hannah*	<u>Maybe</u> cos she's like a big girl, a bit fat cos she's having a baby?
33	*Anna*	<u>I wonder</u> why she's got those things on the end (*points*).
34	*Hannah*	That is just means it's like a little posh boat.
35	*Anna*	I think that's a light (*points*).
36	*Hannah*	It is a light.
37	*Anna*	I think she needs it because . . . Why does she need it . . . if she's got some candles?
38	*Hannah*	<u>Maybe</u> cos the candles aren't . . . like . . . working very well?

Initially the girls make suggestions about the text and try to resolve their questions through explanations (about the muddy skirt). Anna takes more of a lead in the discussion by starting a series of dialogic chains of thinking with questions starting with 'I wonder'. These exchanges occur after the initial line of enquiry related to the muddy skirt, and then form a pattern of exchange, with Hannah responding with possibilities, in particular using 'probably' or 'maybe' to suggest ideas; Anna picks up on the use of 'probably' at the end of the extract. The whole vignette illustrates the notion of provisional meaning and shows the tentative exploration of ideas, with an easy movement with several strands of thinking. Other rationalizing language such as 'cos' (because), 'so' and 'if' are used to maintain the dialogic space of possibility and can be seen to indicate a more exploratory form of co-construction. This is also suggested by the research of Mercer and colleagues in their quantitative analysis of the language of exploratory talk (Mercer et al., 1999; Mercer, 2004; Mercer and Littleton, 2007). However, a close analysis of the other vignettes in the study shows that whereas the children use language markers to frame their discussion and fall into patterns of speech, these do not necessarily indicate a more open, provisional or exploratory element to their discussion, and so may not be indicators of a particular mode of talk.

Liam and James are also in Y1 and in their discussion of the animated film *Otherwise* they seem to vie for the space to speak, with James in particular falling into a pattern of speech when discussing the film. Arguably, this actually constrains the possibility of exploratory ideas as the pattern becomes more rigid as the discussion develops. In the film, a chameleon tries to befriend a group of lizards who blame him when an eagle attacks one of them. The chameleon saves the day by rescuing the captured lizard. In the sequence below, James initially battles for a chance to share his ideas by trying to interrupt Liam's train of thinking:

01 James   Why did the chameleons get the um, that brown (*gestures to head*), the brown lizard?

02 Liam   Er . . . because I think they were mean at the beginning (*looks to door*).

03 James   Yeah because the . . . (*pulls L to face him*) . . . because the eagle came, and they um . . . the eagle, um for the . . . um, (*under breath*) what (*shows flying motion with hand*) um . . .

04 Liam   [Yeah] um it might of not no . . . noticed (*also using arm to show flying*), um the green ones, and then um it wanted to go to the green ones . . .

05 James   [Because it . . .] (*pointing*)

06 Liam   . . . and then it um want going to um the green ones and then . . .

07 James   [Because it . . .]

08 Liam   . . . get the green ones cos um it thought um the green ones were better

09 James   Becau . . . I know why the eagle went for the green ones . . .

10 Liam   Because um . . .

11 James   Because he didn't like the brown ones.

12 Liam   (*coughs*) . . . no . . . (*long pause*) And I know why um . . . they were friends at the end, because um, um um the um, the um one that um, the red one . . .

By initially asking a 'why' question, James appears to be opening up a thinking space, which is then responded to by Liam's 'because' comment. What happens then, through a connection of actions and words (and demonstrating the importance of indicating movements as well as words in the transcript), is a retelling of the part in the story where an eagle attacks the group of green chameleons, ignoring the brown lizard. Liam does not relinquish his control of the floor and James is left to try to interrupt. 'Because' becomes a marker of interjection, and when it is successful (in line 09) he stops, and starts a new idea, rather than completing an explanation. However, this time, rather than asking the question 'why', which generated a space for Liam to speak, he makes a statement, 'I know why . . . ', which enables him to retain the floor and continue the retelling. The function of the word 'because' has been an interruption, not rationalization or explanation. He then continues to use 'I know why . . . ' as a phrase throughout the discussion and it becomes a pattern of speech.

13	James	Yeah?
14	Liam	Saved the, saved the other green ones so then they became friends.
15	James	Yeah . . . (*nods*) um I know why the eagle went the green ones because the green ones were . . . Look! (*L is not looking*) . . . saying, if they had because they didn't want to get um the green ones because they were friendly, but he was trying to pretend they weren't friendly.
16	Liam	(*nods*) Yeah.
17	James	And the other one was good . . . um the brown one didn't want to get killed, it was in the water and relaxed, and they and he didn't want to get killed or bitten on his back, did he? Cos the eagle was biting on his back.
18	Liam	Yep (*now looking away completely*)
19	James	So um (*whispers*) what do you want to say?
20	Liam	(*looks unsure*) Er . . . nothing.
21	James	Um cos er, if the . . . I know why the brown one went up to those rocks cos he knew the green one was gonna kill the um brown . . . green . . . the brown one because he . . . um . . . cos (*L is not making eye contact*) . . . he wanted to be friendly to them and they um but the green ones didn't like him, but when they went up to the . . . the circle, (*unclear*) straw . . .
22	Liam	When they were friends . . .
23	James	(*Gesticulates to interrupt*) [oh yeah!]
24	Liam	. . . When they were friends, and the one knocked um, the other good one out of . . . the other one out of the nest, um the bird flied away and then um they went and um they went off (*gesticulates*) 'fwwwoo' and um another one um went up into the nest um he um holded the hand, he holded um the other ones hand (*holds out arm, gesticulates pulling*) pulled him down and then they lived together.
25	James	How do you know why . . . they lived together cos we didn't see that bit when they lived together well . . . ?
26	Liam	[Yeah . . .]

27 *James* [When] they went up to the nest . . .
28 *Liam*   [They] were friends . . . remember.
29 *James* They went up to the nest, he was trying not to get killed and the green ones were very (*L gestures frantically*) not very nice, so he went up to the rocks and he scared the bird away and then the um green . . .
30 *Liam*   [Then they became friends]
31 *James* . . . the other three went away to go back to their home and the other one, he wanted to live with them and it all lived happily ever after.
32 *Liam*   (*smiles and eye contact, nods*) yeah.
33 *James* Finished?
34 *Liam*   Yeah, are you finished?
35 *James* Yeah. Okay!

As the dialogue continues, James gains more confidence in his retelling, and Liam begins to lose interest, much to James' frustration who tries to command his attention (line 15). After an awkward break (lines 18–20), James continues and finally Liam rejoins the conversation in line 22. James uses his phrase as a question (line 25) to challenge Liam's assumption that they all lived together at the end, by asking: 'How do you know why . . . ?' This has the impact of allowing James to regain the floor and continue his retelling, with Liam able only to repeat his point that the lizards were friends.

As part of their sociocultural discourse analysis Mercer et al. (1999) and later Mercer and Littleton (2007) drew on quantitative word indicators to define 'exploratory' talk. In their research, words such as 'I think', 'I agree' and 'because' were identified as indicators of an exploratory mode of talking. However, in this study the Liam and James vignette illustrates that what may appear to be an indicator of a particular mode of talking – that is, the use of the word 'because' – may actually be serving a different purpose of gaining or holding the floor, particularly when used repeatedly and with 'I know why'. This highlights the importance of a qualitative approach as recognized by Mercer (2004), as it allows for the function of language markers to be analyzed, not just their frequency.

There are also indications in the vignettes that the individual markers of the language of possibility may encompass a frequency of words that are non-specific in meaning. There is a high frequency of the word 'like', and use of the phrase 'kind of', which almost take on a structural function, demarcating a space in thinking or a 'pause' in which to prepare a thought, but use of these words is interesting. Suggesting that something is 'like' something else, or 'kind of', is being indefinite and therefore is open to challenges or alternatives. However, it is important to note that in the vignette of Sophie and Gina's discussion of Magritte's *Golconde* (Y6), the use of the word 'like' becomes part of their pattern of dialogue very quickly, though more predominantly by Sophie:

01 *Sophie* That's really actually quite strange.
02 *Gina*   Yeah . . . there's lots of men and they kind of [seem to be] . . .
03 *Sophie* [Reminds me of] Mary Poppins . . .

04	*Gina*	Hmm, but a male version . . .
05	*Sophie*	. . . of Mary Poppins.
06	*Gina*	And houses . . .
07	*Sophie*	It's <u>like</u> and <u>like</u> they're <u>like</u> just falling down.
08	*Gina*	[mmm] Just falling from the sky . . .
09	*Sophie*	[<u>Like</u>] it's quite . . .
10	*Gina*	It really is raining men . . . (*smiles*)
11	*Sophie*	(*smiles*) yeah.
12	*Gina*	Cos I thought that <u>like</u>, one or two of them had umbrellas, but it's just all loads and loads of others in the background.
13	*Sophie*	Yeah just loads and loads and loads <u>like</u> . . . they're <u>like</u> . . . I wonder what's over those houses, <u>like</u> over them cos there's like men in the distance so . . . I wonder where they're gonna land but you tell that he's gonna land like there or (*points*) that one's gonna land there, and that one's gonna land of top of him (*looks at G – G smiles, both half laugh*).
14	*Gina*	I like that picture.
15	*Sophie*	Yeah . . . Look there are all the little chimneys in the background . . .
16	*Gina*	Or are they people actually falling? (*points and laughs*)
17	*Sophie*	Oh yeah they could be! Look there!
18	*Gina*	Oh yeah, I think they're actually people falling . . .
19	*Sophie*	(*unclear – covering mouth and G is talking at the same time*)
20	*Gina*	. . . those grey things are the chimneys.
21	*Sophie*	What if there's a lake?
22	*Gina*	And they might go falling into it . . .

The structural function of these words provides a secure frame in which the dialogue can function, without the need for a definite idea, but this does not mean that the critical and creative thinking that occurs within these dialogues is particularly sophisticated. In fact, in the vignette of Tilly and Kate (also Y6), while Tilly demonstrates sophisticated structural language, her ideas do not extend far beyond the literal interpretations of the picturebook *Way Home*. She displays language that seems to be setting up sophisticated reflective thinking (underlined below), yet does not then follow this with creative and divergent solutions, rather a series of observations about the text:

06	*Tilly*	But um <u>I thought that, compared or in relation to</u> any other books I've read, it was quite unusual? Because . . . um . . . the way it was written<u>?</u>
07	*Kate*	Yeah.
08	*Tilly*	And I actually quite liked the story at the end.
09	*Kate*	I loved the pictures in it [yeah] . . . look these . . . look there's just so much detail in them.
10	*Tilly*	[Yeah].
11	*Kate*	And . . . um I really like the uh, like this one here, um where's it gone (*searches through pages*) This one here with the shadows and everything.
12	*Tilly*	[yeah . . . <u>I think</u>]
13	*Kate*	And that one . . . I like that one.

14 *Tilly* Definitely, yeah.
15 *Kate* That one's very good as well, because like it's a sky view.
16 *Tilly* Yeah.
17 *Kate* I think they're all really good.
18 *Tilly* I think it's quite like, somehow its . . .
19 *Kate* . . . quite abstract
20 *Tilly* Yeah . . . I'm just wondering, like, um, all about him, like does he have
          family? Does he actually have a real home? All these questions were
          like popping into my head.
21 *Kate* [Yes] Yeah and like . . . does he, like, (*looks at camera*) does he want
          to . . . does he think it's like kitten is like his friend or a pet? Is it like
          the kitten is his friend or like just a pet?
22 *Tilly* [Yeah] . . . yeah it's kind of like, it makes me feel (unclear) is he actu-
          ally lonely?
23 *Kate* Yeah
24 *Tilly* Cos you wouldn't, I personally wouldn't, if I didn't have a friends, I
          just wouldn't pick up a cat, you know, that's me, but . . .

The effect of this vague language is that Kate merely agrees to each of the statements or continues the observations about the quality of the pictures. A number
of variables may affect this discussion. It could be that the text does not sufficiently
provoke a divergent response, or that they are overly conscious of the task, and
the fact that they are being recorded, or the relationship between the two children
may be awkward. Therefore, the judgements about this discussion are not judgements made about the children, but serve to illustrate and develop the theory that
particular linguistic markers are used to both create and maintain a dialogic space
of possibility.

When looking closely at the patterns of language that the children use, it can
be seen that there are patterns of hypothetical linguistic markers, but these are not
entirely consistent, and this again highlights the danger of a purely quantitative
analysis of talk. From the vignettes analyzed above, it appears that the functions
of individual words vary between individual co-constructive dialogues, and that
while some broad categories of function may be allocated to specific linguistic
markers, this may not always be the case. The children demonstrate a sophisticated
use of these markers, both creating their own repetitions and using key indicators for alternative purposes (for example, Liam and James). Sometimes they use
the apparent language of co-construction to create the illusion that their dialogue
contains more complex thinking than is actually evident (as seen in the vignette of
Tilly and Kate). Through this they are showing an orientation towards the completion of the task, with little self-reflection on the value of their ideas.

Critical and creative thinking in dialogic chains

Across the whole data set, there are a total of 52 different dialogic chains of thinking. For Harry and Ben (10 of the chains), as explored in the previous chapter, these

most often start with a question, a high indicator of creative thinking (Burnard et al., 2006). Of the remaining 42 chains, 25 start with a question or suggestion. However, a further 16 of the chains are initiated by a statement, which in itself appears to leaves no room for provisional meaning or potential, unless followed up in the same turn by a more divergent move. Neither do most of the statement initiations lead to a question or a suggestion from the other speaker. The impact this has on the dialogue can be explored by looking closely at an example where there is a predominance of initiations that indicate divergent thinking (Hannah and Anna), and in comparison, an example where there is a predominance of statements deemed to indicate more convergent thinking used as initiations (Liam and James). Both pairs of children are from Y1. In the sequence below, Hannah and Anna discuss why the Lady of Shalott's skirt seems to be hanging over the side of the boat:

03	Hannah	While she's sailing on the boat . . . Why's her skirt hanging out in the water?
04	Anna	I don't know, probably she just wants to get her skirt wet so she can dry it, so, cos she, look it's quite muddy isn't it? (*Points at screen*)
05	Hannah	Mm
06	Anna	It's quite muddy.
07	Hannah	Maybe it's muddy cos she [went] . . .
08	Anna	[Went] in the mud.
09	Hannah	Yeah then she needs like, like went on the boat and she like hanged it [over in the water] . . .
10	Anna	[Yeah, so, what]
11	Hannah	. . . to clean it all up.

The extract shows a complete dialogic chain of thinking, as they then move on to talk about whether the Lady has a belt on her skirt which, while related, is not specifically about her clothes being muddy. However, the children return to the subject of muddy clothes a few lines later:

16	Anna	Yeah <u>I wonder</u> why she needs to clean her dress, cos . . .
17	Hannah	<u>Maybe</u> she like fell over in the mud cos she probably tripped over a stone or a [ ] and she . . . flat into the mud (*gestures*).
18	Anna	She could put it in a dishwasher couldn't she?
19	Hannah	(*Laughs*) . . . Dishwasher?!
20	Anna	(*Laughs*) No I mean a . . . thingy!

Both sequences start with a question, which provides the respondent the opportunity to make a suggestion, which is then answered with another suggestion or explanation. This can be termed as 'possibility thinking' (Craft, 2000) and it involves the creation of a narrative that sits outside the given text. It also allows both children to join together to co-construct meaning from the picture, and they both make suggestions and ask questions. They use the dialogic space of possibility to extend each other's ideas and find a solution to the problem that they have found: why material appears to be hanging over the side of the boat. However, asking questions or making suggestions does not necessarily mean a longer chain of dialogue related to one theme, and thereby a deeper or wider engagement with the thinking as seen in Harry and Ben's discussions. Many of the chains in the vignette of Hannah and Anna are very short: out of a total of 11 chains, over half of them are three turns or less. They seem to move from idea to idea until they find one that they both want to develop. Towards the end of their discussion, there are three new ideas generated in quick succession but none of them provide sufficient interest in the respondent to generate a long chain of thinking.

31	*Anna*	Um, <u>I wonder</u> what . . . um . . . <u>I wonder</u> why she's got a big boat not a little rowing boat.
32	*Hannah*	<u>Maybe</u> cos she's like a big girl, a bit fat cos she's having a baby?
33	*Anna*	<u>I wonder</u> why she's got those things on the end (*points*).
34	*Hannah*	That is just means it's like a little posh boat.
35	*Anna*	I think that's a light (*points*).

While Hannah responds to the initiation (line 32), Anna does not continue the line of thinking she has initiated; she abandons it and starts with a new question or suggestion (line 33). This brings to mind the analogy of a tennis match, with each player either hitting the ball too wide (therefore making it non-returnable) or simply not returning the ball at all. It is the respondent who chooses whether to keep the rally going or to abandon it and start afresh. It is interesting that in the example above, it was the initiator of the line of enquiry, Anna, who chose to continue the discussion by asking a new question. Remembering the prompts that the children were given to complete the task, it could be argued that they are doing as they have been directed, asking questions. However, there is ample evidence within the same vignette (the examples above relating to the muddy skirt in particular) that the children are willing and able to move a question into a generation of creative and critical co-construction of meaning, to find solutions as well as problems.

In the other example, Liam and James discuss the animated film *Otherwise*. In their exchanges their creative thinking is also limited by the moves they make. They start by asking a question about the text, which opens a range of possible moves that can be made. However, they quickly move into an exchange of statements as they retell the story:

21	*James*	Um cos er, if the . . . I know why the brown one went up to those rocks cos he knew the green one was gonna kill the um brown . . . green . . . the brown one because he . . . um . . . cos (*L is not making eye contact*) . . . he wanted to be friendly to them and they um but the green ones didn't like him, but when they went up to the . . . the circle, (unclear) straw . . .
22	*Liam*	When they were friends . . .

23	James	(*Gesticulates to interrupt*) [oh yeah!]
24	Liam	. . . When they were friends, and the one knocked um, the other good one out of . . . the other one out of the nest, um the bird flied away and then um they went and um they went off (*gesticulates*) 'fwwwoo' and um another one um went up into the nest um he um holded the hand, he holded um the other ones hand (*holds out arm, gesticulates pulling*) pulled him down and then they lived together.
25	James	How do you know why . . . they lived together cos we didn't see that bit when they lived together well . . . ?
26	Liam	[Yeah . . .]
27	James	[When] they went up to the nest . . .
28	Liam	[They] were friends . . . remember.
29	James	They went up to the nest, he was trying not to get killed and the green ones were very (*L gestures frantically*) not very nice, so he went up to the rocks and he scared the bird away and then the um green . . .
30	Liam	[Then they became friends]
31	James	. . . the other three went away to go back to their home and the other one, he wanted to live with them and it all lived happily ever after.
32	Liam	(*smiles and eye contact, nods*) yeah.

In this sequence of 12 turns, the dialogue is dominated by a retelling of the narrative with the only questions that are raised being those seeking clarification from the other child. The statement moves do not lead to hypothesis but to agreement, or continuation, and neither child moves beyond these convergent styles in the same way that Harry and Ben do when discussing their visual text.

What is noticeable in comparison to the Hannah and Anna extract is the length of each turn. Both boys speak at length to tell their part of the narrative or to explain it, and they move together to the end of the story, passing the narrative between them, but not generating any possibilities outside the world of the text other than the idea that all the animals lived together at the end. In fact, this is an interesting interjection by Liam, as James very quickly dismisses it as not based on the evidence in the film:

| 25 | James | How do you know why . . . they lived together cos we didn't see that bit when they lived together well . . . ? |

By stating that ' . . . we didn't see that bit', he is grounding the co-construction of meaning firmly within the world of the text and not accepting or promoting ideas that are extensions of the 'story world', as described by Anderson et al. (2001). This concept of narrative creation and extension beyond what is presented in the text is explored more fully in the next chapter when the creative comprehension strategies the children use to engage with the text are highlighted.

From these two examples it could be argued that, within this particular context, sequences that start from a divergent point, by raising questions or suggestions, are more likely to generate creative and critical co-constructive thinking.

However, the case of Sophie and Gina disproves this as they start their thinking from a range of different moves. In their discussion of the Magritte picture *Golconde*, they engage in 11 different dialogic chains of thinking, of which six are initiated by either suggestions or questions. The other four initiations are statements. Within their discussion they move through ideas related to both where the men are going to land and where they have come from. They discuss whether it is 'raining men' (both laughing at the cultural connection to a 1980s pop song) or whether it is an illusion. The starting point of each chain of thinking does not seem to impact on its length or the type of co-constructive moves that happen within it. The moves, too, are equally spread as there are no definite patterns of move sequence. The only pattern that is discernible from the whole episode is that whereas they start their discussion mainly using statements as initiations, they increasingly use questions or suggestions. For example, in this first sequence from the start of their discussion, they make general statements about the picture, identifying features in it. However, creative thinking is still enabled by these statements and their co-construction leads to two divergent cultural connections, of *Mary Poppins* and *It's Raining Men*:

01	*Sophie*	That's really actually quite strange.
02	*Gina*	Yeah . . . there's lots of men and they kind of [seem to be] . . .
03	*Sophie*	[Reminds me of] Mary Poppins . . .
04	*Gina*	Hmm, but a male version . . .
05	*Sophie*	. . . of Mary Poppins.
06	*Gina*	And houses . . .
07	*Sophie*	It's like and like they're like just falling down.
08	*Gina*	[mmm] Just falling from the sky . . .
09	*Sophie*	[Like] it's quite . . .
10	*Gina*	It really is raining men . . . (*smiles*)
11	*Sophie*	(*smiles*) yeah.
12	*Gina*	Cos I thought that like, one or two of them had umbrellas, but it's just all loads and loads of others in the background.

In the sequence below, from later in their discussion where they explore where the people in the picture have come from, they generate different ideas by suggesting or asking questions, and equally they are able to engage in creative/divergent thinking:

40	*Gina*	I wonder like how they like kind of fell from in the first place?
41	*Sophie*	Yeah it's like someone dropping them or something.
42	*Gina*	Like if you could look up into the sky in that picture and then you could actually see where they were falling from, or if they were just appearing.
43	*Sophie*	Yeah . . . or is it just like natural . . . like it always happens (*G smiles and shakes head – half laughs*)? So it's not (*looks at camera*) . . . really . . . real. Well it's like . . . it could be an illusion?
44	*Gina*	Could be . . .
45	*Sophie*	Or it could just be that man, printed again and again.

As children in Y6, it could be argued that Sophie and Gina are able to maintain a more sophisticated approach to the task. However, Harry and Ben in Y1 discuss the same picture and demonstrate a different though arguably equally sophisticated approach.

All of the above examples show that while the analysis of Harry and Ben's discussion presents a clear picture of how a space for creative and divergent thinking is created (that is, through question raising or suggestions), this is seen not to be the case in the rest of the vignettes, as any of the possible co-constructive moves could create such a space. The movement into creative co-constructive thinking is dependent on the response rather than the initiation.

Seeking resolution

Harry and Ben's discussions illustrate that some co-constructive moves are seemingly more convergent and solution-finding (for example, rationalizing or making a statement). However, this does not necessarily mean that they are less likely to stimulate a connected response. Equally, the dialogic chains of thinking that Harry and Ben follow do not often finish with a clear resolution, but are more often left in a state of possibility. Coding their dialogue shows that they can move fluidly from a state of apparent resolution into a continuation of an idea, or conversely leave an idea open and move onto a new line of enquiry. They seem to be quite happy to leave the meanings provisional. The prompts for the task may have led the children to this, and this supports the findings of Corden (2000) who suggests that children respond in a more exploratory way when they feel that their teachers are more interested in the process than the product of their discussions. When they are clear that the task is open, they are keen to persevere with it, and able to regulate their engagement. This is also emphasized by Nystrand et al. (1997) who suggest that while discussion tasks should have clear parameters, teachers should avoid telling children exactly 'how to proceed' (1997: 102). From this perspective, and to refer back to Hymes' (1972) work, the communicative 'situation', or sociocultural context, can be seen to directly influence the mode of talk. A goal-orientated classroom context would be more concerned with finding the correct answer than exploring possibilities. On the other hand, a communicative situation geared towards exploring possible meanings, with a teacher valuing the process of this co-construction, would promote this exploration. There are several writers (for example Smith, 2010; Swain, 2010) who argue that teachers should not only provide these opportunities for children to explore their responses to text, but that they should also actively model critical and creative language, making explicit the skills that they are using.

However, that the children move so easily from idea to idea with no apparent clear 'answer' found is interesting and worthy of exploration through the data. When the chains of dialogue in the vignettes of Hannah and Anna and Sophie and Gina are analyzed to show the move that 'completes' each chain before the talk moves to a new idea, the most frequently occurring moves are rationalizations or explanations. This would suggest that these children seem more inclined to offer a solution before moving onto another line of enquiry, which is particularly borne out by the fact that for Anna and Hannah, every new chain of thinking starts with either a suggestion or a question. However, in this extract from the final part of their dialogue, it can be seen that this does not mean that they explore the ideas in any depth as while questions are raised and suggestions made, the resulting explanation does not lead to a widening or deepening of ideas, but rather to a new question or suggestion. They seem to seek many explanations for different parts of the visual text, rather than one overarching interpretation. The start of each new dialogic chain of thinking is marked as **DCT**:

31	*Anna*	**DCT1** Um, I wonder what . . . um . . . I wonder why she's got a big boat not a little rowing boat.
32	*Hannah*	Maybe cos she's like a big girl, a bit fat cos she's having a baby?
33	*Anna*	**DCT2** I wonder why she's got those things on the end (*points*).
34	*Hannah*	That is just means it's like a little posh boat.
35	*Anna*	**DCT3** I think that's a light (*points*).
36	*Hannah*	It is a light.
37	*Anna*	I think she needs it because . . . Why does she need it . . . if she's got some candles?
38	*Hannah*	Maybe cos the candles aren't . . . like . . . working very well?

In Sophie and Gina's discussion, the explanations are tied more closely to the content of the text, as opposed to the extension of the text-world more apparent in the discussion between Hannah and Anna. They often provide explanations for their suggestions, and in some cases continue their explanation across two turns of speech. This is illustrated by an extract from the middle of their dialogue in which there are three dialogic chains of thinking (demarcated within the transcript):

30	*Gina*	**DCT1** So you get the phrase, it's raining cats and dogs . . .
31	*Sophie*	[Yeah]
32	*Gina*	. . . when it's just raining loads, but you don't get 'raining men' much as a phrase.
33	*Sophie*	Unless it's a song, but, (*gestures*) but . . . **DCT2** I wonder what's over there . . . could be like . . . magic. (*looks at G*)
34	*Gina*	Yeah, cos if, but I don't think there's like any buildings the same as that down there . . . cos otherwise . . .
35	*Sophie*	[Could be like totally different]
36	*Gina*	They'd be landing on . . . the roof, but that's going down, so could be . . . [not the same building]
37	*Sophie*	[Flat roofs, could be flat roofs . . . **DCT3** Could be a totally differ-ent . . . land basically.
38	*Gina*	Mmm (*looks doubtful*)
39	*Sophie*	Like that's one land and that's another land, and that's another land (*points*).

The chains of thinking start with Gina making a cultural reference to a common rain metaphor (line 30), which she then explains by linking to her earlier reference to a song. Sophie then extends this explanation by making it explicit (line 33), which could be to demonstrate that she understands the reference and can use it too. She then uses her turn to make a new constructive move, starting a new line of enquiry about the landscape of the picture, which Gina then develops by suggesting that there wouldn't be any buildings (line 34). At this point the speech overlaps and Gina continues her explanation of why there would be no buildings in the distance. Simultaneously, Sophie has developed her line of thinking to suggest that this could be a different land altogether, though she responds first to Gina's comment about roofs, then continues her suggestion that the scene is from another land (line 37). Sophie's response is uncertain, signified by both her speech, 'Mmm . . . ', and her expression of doubt, and Gina continues to explain her suggestion.

An interesting feature of these vignettes, however, is that in both cases, across the whole of their discussion, the children return to a previously discussed idea. For Hannah and Anna this means coming back to the idea of the Lady of Shalott's muddy skirt, and for Sophie and Gina, the inter-subjective reference to the song *It's Raining Men*. In both cases this is instigated by the child whose idea it originally was, so it is Anna who returns to the theme of the muddy skirt, and Gina who repeats the reference to *It's Raining Men*. There could be several reasons for this, but, as a function of co-constructive talk, it can be seen as serving the purpose of returning to a more secure idea between the co-constructions of new ideas, which may not be as successful. Although the data set is clearly too small to be able to make any clear comparison between the Y1 and Y6 children, it is hard to ignore the ease with which the Y1 children move creatively beyond the frame of the text compared with their Y6 counterparts, particularly when responding to the same text stimulus.

Harry and Ben's co-construction sees them moving towards a resolution (that of helicopters, or catching a fish for tea). Other vignettes illustrate a model of talk where the first idea may actually be the preferred resolution and so recurs. The resolution, then, may not actually occur at the end of the discussion, arrived at through a neatly linear journey. The 'cycles' (Sinclair and Coulthard, 1975: 12) of meaning can occur and recur and the individual chains of thinking or lines of enquiry result in varying degrees of convergence. In the vignette of Alex and Sam discussing the text *Way Home*, there are two recurrent ideas they pursue through their entire dialogue, but these are quickly established as the most significant ideas in the text. The first is related to the protagonist, Shane's, homelessness and the other is related to the theme of cats. They move between these ideas fluently and develop them both through a series of linked chains of thinking. Table 4.1 shows their entire discussion with the two main strands of thinking organized into two columns, and a third column for comments that served to maintain the dialogue itself rather than add to the content of the ideas.

TABLE 4.1 Alex and Sam discuss *Way Home*

Turn	Dialogic maintainers	Shane's homelessness	Cats
01 Alex	That was nothing like I thought it was gonna to be . . .		
		I thought it was gonna like go to a building or something but . . . mmm . . . just went to a cardboard box.	
02 Sam		I thought like he was going like to go to like a really nice house or something like that.	
03 Alex		But then when it got into the middle part, it um like got nearer towards the junk stuff I thought that's turning into . . . er . . . (*pause*)	
			and I think his whole life is devoted to cats.
04 Sam	Mmm		
05 Alex			Cos at the end he had loads of pictures of cats and stuff.
06 Sam			Yeah and there's not much more people there.
07 Alex			And it's a bit weird cos he kept on calling a cat different names and stuff.
08 Sam			Yeah like 'Crazy Cat' . . .
09 Alex			And 'Cat Number One',
10 Sam			'Best cat'
	And um I'm just surprised,	I thought he was like just lost or ran away	
	Um . . . and	(*pause*)	
11 Alex			how did he get that cat in the first place? He like . . .
12 Sam			Look if you go back to the beginning (*flicks pages*) it doesn't tell you how he got it, does it?
13 Alex			Yeah . . . Well it does tell you how he got it.

(*continued*)

14 Sam			(*reading*) . . . Alright . . .
15 Alex			I was a bit surprised the cat went into there, so quickly, without being really scared.
16 Sam			Yeah I know, you walk up to a cat and it just legs it.
17 Alex			Yeah. And he just walked up to it and it went straight into his jacket.
18 Sam			I don't think he . . . I thought it was going to be like, when you saw the picture of the dog.
19 Alex	(unclear)		
20 Sam			yeah . . . I thought he was going to be like really scared and run off.
21 Alex			And then I thought that cat wouldn't come back to him, but . . .
22 Sam			Yeah I think that.
23 Alex			It's weird . . . there it is (*points*) . . .
24 Sam			Yeah, I got, I think that I'd probably leg it as well . . .
25 Alex			Yeah (*both smile*).
26 Sam	Mm . . . and . . .		
27 Alex			I think he had, I think the whole story is like he had a cat before and he wants another one so he gets a stray one, stuff like that.
28 Sam	Mmm . . . and then . . .		
29 Alex	I'm surprised actually.		
30 Sam		You can tell by the first page like he had an alright house but then like near the end . . .	
31 Alex		It's like a cardboard box	
32 Sam		(*laughs*) Yeah . . . when you went from . . . that (*points*) which is nice, to that (*flicks pages*) and then to that . . .	

(*continued*)

TABLE 4.1 *(continued)*

Turn	Dialogic maintainers	Shane's homelessness	Cats
33 Alex		. . . and then to that *(flicks pages)*	
34 Sam			Yeah, reckon like one of the cats must have died and like he wanted to get another one?
35 Alex			Yep or the cat ran away.
36 Sam		I'm just wondering how, why, I'm wondering if he used to have a proper home or something?	
37 Alex		Or he got thrown out cos his mum and dad, wasn't, yeah he like ran away from home and stuff.	
38 Sam		Or he was an orphan.	
39 Alex		Yeah.	

The transcript illustrates how Alex and Sam negotiate the co-construction of meaning in a far more complex way than Hannah and Anna, who neatly move from a 'question/suggestion to explanation' pattern of divergent thinking. Alex and Sam are able to explore two ideas at once, both creatively, by providing explanations that reside beyond the world of the text. They provide an explanation for why Shane picks up the cat, and also for why he might be homeless. Towards the end in particular, they move between both ideas, making meaning from the text by divergently exploring possibilities without breaking the fluency of their co-construction. Their two main themes are explored concurrently and recurrently, and they are able to manage these parallel strands.

It can be argued that there are two moments of possible resolution: first within the dialogue as a whole meaning-making event, and second within each new dialogic chain of thinking as a micro-meaning event; that is, a small co-constructive part in a larger whole. In the vignettes, the children focus on a few key ideas to which they return, though may leave ultimately unresolved. In none of the vignettes do the children define the conclusion of the task as a resolution point. Rather, they seem to continue talking until there are no more ideas and either just stop talking, or mark the end of the discussion formally as in this example by Liam and James:

33 James Finished?
34 Liam Yeah, are you finished?
35 James Yeah. Okay!

The children do not always move towards a clear resolution and may find that their most central and agreeable idea or solution happens towards the start of their dialogue, and several smaller dialogic chains of thinking exist within the wider frame of the whole discussion. The co-constructive moves that constitute these chains of thinking can be viewed as potentially divergent or convergent, though even a seemingly closed statement can lead to an extension or agreement by the other speaker. Furthermore, in each of the vignettes, a key idea is returned to later on, usually by the speaker who initiated it.

Chapter summary

This chapter has explored the critical and creative thinking that is evident in the children's discussions about text. Analyzing their talk, the language of critical and creative thinking could be seen to be indicated through linguistic markers, though these were not always consistent. Some co-constructive moves appear to generate more creative thinking, particularly through the use of questioning or making suggestions, and some moves seem more convergent, offering explanation or rationalizing ideas proposed. Whatever the potential of the move to think of possibilities or to propel towards resolution, it is the respondent's choice of move that steers the discussion. Not all divergent creative thinking leads to resolution in a linear fashion. Ideas may be recurrent, or concurrent, and resolution may occur and quickly be followed by a new idea or new dialogic chain of thinking.

5

READING TOGETHER

Transactional strategies for making meaning

'Reading is not the discovery of meaning . . . but the creation of it.'

(Benton, 2004: 114)

Making meaning from text as a critical and creative cognitive process

The previous chapter explored the critical and creative-thinking processes apparent in the children's language as they talked together to make meaning from text. These processes were recognized for their divergent and convergent properties of problem-solving and seeking resolution to hypotheses. This chapter now explores the process of meaning-making more deeply, considering the reading comprehension strategies that the children use but also setting these dialogic transactions between text and readers in the context of creative/divergent and critical/convergent thinking.

In Chapter 2, a sociocultural perspective on reading was given, situating each reading event as uniquely positioned in time and space and highlighting the importance of schema (or the reader's own existing understandings about the patterns and connections of the world) in making connections between oneself as a reader and the text. While the perspectives have changed over time, moving from reading as a 'psycholinguistic guessing game' (Goodman, 1967) through to sociolinguistic and sociocultural models (Pearson, 2009), there is basic agreement about what constitutes reading comprehension, even if much of the research is geared towards the teaching or instruction of the skills or transactional strategies of reading (for example, Dole et al., 1991, Pressley, 2000; Pearson, 2009; Wolf et al., 2005). Researchers who have investigated transactional strategy instruction, such as Palincsar and Brown (1984), Pressley (2006) and Keene and Zimmerman (1997), propose models of reading comprehension that present a detailed analysis of the cognitive strategies employed by effective readers of text. Keene and Zimmerman view reading as an 'individual mosaic' with their research conducted through reader workshops initially in the 1990s in which, similarly to the research of Palincsar and Brown in the 1980s, the children engaged in text are involved in a collaborative reading event. While Palincsar and Brown concentrated on four strategies (summarizing, clarifying, questioning and predicting), Keene and Zimmerman pose six common features of effective reading comprehension: metacognition, determining importance, questioning, evoking images, inferences and synthesis. In addition to these, Pressley (2006) identifies using prior knowledge and interpreting strategies, while the work of Lewis and Tregenza (2007) highlights the importance of empathy in engagement with text. This links to reader response theories (for example Protherough, 1983) in considering the dynamic of engagement (Maine and Waller, 2011). More recent cognitive theories of children's literature extend this by considering 'theory of mind' and the ability to step into the shoes of characters (Nikolajeva, 2014) as important parts of engagement or 'entanglement' (Iser, 1978) with text. Drawing all of the strategies together and mapping them as critical or creative thinking supports the notion of opening a dialogic space for meaning-making through asking questions and making hypotheses, and closing it through seeking resolutions and explanations. The strategies are also potentially indicated through specific linguistic markers that are evident in the children's talk.

First, the transactional strategy of *questioning* is highlighted in the work of several writers (as discussed in Smith, 1985, 1988; Palincsar and Brown, 1984; Pressley, 2006; Lewis and Tregenza, 2007). Keene and Zimmerman argue that proficient readers understand that questions deepen understanding, but also that they often lead to more questions. This relates to the research of Burnard et al. (2006) who found questioning a key element of possibility thinking. As a comprehension strategy, therefore, it can be classified as divergent, and is indicated by linguistic markers such as 'What is . . . ?' and 'Why . . . ?' or questions preceded by 'I wonder . . . '. In their research, Soter et al. (2008) categorize questions as 'authentic' or 'non-authentic', recognizing the difference between questions that propelled comprehension forward and those that were 'test' questions perhaps more readily associated with teaching. A teacherly stance is sometimes adopted by one of the children in the reading pairs. This is most notable in Harry's discussion, as he takes control of the task from the start, positioning himself in an authoritative role and asking Ben teacherly questions. 'Right, what do you think it is first?' he challenges when discussing *The Lady of Shalott*. This positioning perhaps indicates something about his understanding of the task and his management of it – both points to be returned to in the next chapter.

Asking questions leads to hypothesis or *prediction*, which Smith (1985, 1988) argues are at the heart of the connection to existing schema. He defines prediction as the 'prior elimination of unlikely alternatives' (1985: 82) to hypothesize what will happen next. Palincsar and Brown (1984) also include prediction as a key aspect of reading comprehension. However, the difficulty with the term prediction is the implication that something is going to happen next, in a linear text with a temporal pathway (Kress and van Leeuwen, 1996). A multi-modal view of reading includes more than just verbal text, and the texts may be spatial with no linear pathway. In later work, Palincsar defines prediction as the development of a hypothesis to be tested as the reading progresses (2003: 101). This definition allows for the accommodation of non-verbal text and suggests the question of 'what might be?' rather than 'what happens next?'. However, the concept of 'testing the hypothesis' as the reading progresses remains problematic, as there may be no further clarification that a hypothesis is correct other than through rationalization and justification on the part of the reader. This links to the strong theme of self-monitoring or metacognition, seeking clarification when misunderstanding happens (Palincsar and Brown, 1984; Pressley, 2000, 2006), which is built into theories around reading comprehension and is discussed in detail in the next chapter. Suffice to say here that efficient readers are aware of the process they are engaged in, and monitor themselves throughout to ensure that their interpretations are reasonable.

The third 'divergent' transactional strategy identified by Keene and Zimmerman (1997) is *evoking images*, or as Pressley calls it, 'constructing mental images' (2006: 337). If this is termed 'imagining' then it is clearly a creative-thinking strategy, and links to the idea of image creation identified by Tannen in her work exploring imagery in conversational discourse and the importance of creating images to communicate meaning and then to interpret it. She argues that the creation of images is an important part of co-construction in the roles of both the speaker and the listener. The speaker's description of an image helps the listener to create a similar picture and this leads to a common understanding (Tannen, 1989: 135). Therefore, the 'signs' of words (whether verbal or written) can create a meaning that is visual, and in particular a context in which to make sense of an intended meaning. The listener, or rather respondent, can then creatively embellish the image with their own ideas. Whether a dialogic transaction between two speakers, or a transaction between text and reader, the creation of images is central to the meaning-making process, and so important to identify in the children's discussion. Rather than having a set of specific speech markers to indicate that it is happening, the strategy seems to be apparent when children describe scenes beyond the text as it appears and evoke new images to support their understandings. For example, when Harry and Ben talk about helicopters dropping men from the sky, they are stepping outside the frame of the text and generating new ideas through 'imaginative activity' (National Advisory Committee on Creative and Cultural Education, 1999). An extension to this concept of evoking images is to create narratives that move beyond what is given to explain the text. While these narratives can be seen as creative thinking, they relate to the 'special kind of problem-solving' that Nickerson (1999: 394) describes. The narratives that the children construct (such as the story of the Lady of Shalott taking a cat to catch fish to eat for tea) act as creative solutions to explain the picture. The children are thinking outside the box, or frame, to make sense of it.

The strategy of inference or interpreting (Pressley, 2006) can also be argued to be a divergent and creative strategy. It involves making connections between what is known and what the text might suggest, and offers a multitude of possibilities, as it requires the blending of text and personal experience. Again linked to schema, this strategy is indicative of reading as a unique and personal experience. The identification of specific speech markers for this is a more problematic issue. It can be linked to the suggestion or positing of theories, the potentiating language of possibility that the children use: 'I think . . . because . . . ', 'mightn't it . . . ?' and 'that reminds me of . . . '. These suggest the creative cognitive process of making links, but also with the dialogic function of offering a possibility for discussion. Harry and Ben infer that there must be some way that the people are arriving at their positions in the sky in *Golconde*; that there must be something beyond the frame causing the situation that is seen. They judge the credibility of their suggestions. Both of these skills are identified by Ennis (1987) and Quellmalz (1987) as part of the critical-thinking process. Harry challenges Ben to explain how one helicopter could hold all the people in the picture, suggesting it is not a credible response. However, Ben then justifies his position by arguing that there could be many helicopters, and Harry, 'judging the adequacy of the solution' (Quellmalz, 1987: 89), extends the notion of a few more than 'one' into a bigger solution (the number of the helicopters is so great it needs to be counted in 'tens'). All of these complex critical-thinking processes take place within a few lines of dialogue, demonstrating the richness and complexity of the processes in which the children are engaged.

Determining importance revolves around reasoning and justifying. It can be tied together with the use of prior knowledge and schema as a strategy, as it is only through connecting to what is known, either about the word or other texts, that the importance of features in the new text can be determined. This focusing might occur throughout a discussion, though when used initially it helps the dialogic readers to target their discussion. For Alex and Sam, who keep returning to the themes of homelessness and cats, the strategy allows them to continue to extend their thinking around the themes they find most interesting. Quellmalz (1987) describes the first step in the critical-thinking process as identifying or formulating questions. This is not the same as asking a question; it is a step before, the decision to focus attention on one area. If determining importance is seen as a key comprehension strategy for linear verbal texts, then this is even more apparent when readers are deciphering an ambiguous visual text and deciding a reading pathway towards meaning. As the objects within an image are 'simultaneously present' (Kress, 2003: 20), the readers must determine the importance of the objects that they see to decide which is most significant. The Waterhouse picture (discussed by Harry and Ben and Anna and Hannah) has a central object that is a figure, yet Harry and Ben hardly discuss her, being more interested in the surrounding water or the boat. In the Magritte picture, Harry and Ben settle on the importance of the figures, yet become more interested in the possible action outside the frame.

Pressley (2000) asserts that 'weak' readers may not necessarily be able to judge the relevance of accessed prior knowledge. That is, if inappropriate importance is given to an object or idea within a text, this may lead the children towards irrelevent solutions. Perhaps Harry and Ben can be seen as weak readers who are unable to decide on the most significant feature of the text. However, a more creative perspective could suggest that they are not bound by rigid cultural and aesthetic assumptions (Barthes, 1977) which lead them to interpret the pictures in a particular way. Rather, their creative curiosity transcends the frame of the picture and they invent possible narratives to explain what they see. The opportunities afforded by situations in which a provisional space of meaning is created are such that the meaning-makers themselves monitor and decide the importance of their construed sense of the text. By offering situations where they can explore meaning and determine importance in a divergent way, and can monitor the assigning of that importance, the activity supports them as independent reflective readers, aware of the choices and decisions they are making.

The final common strategy that researchers investigating transactional strategies identify is *synthesis* (Keene and Zimmerman, 1997) or summarizing (Palincsar and Brown, 1984; Pressley, 2000, 2006), though arguably the latter is a lesser skill than the ability to bring ideas together to form an understanding. Synthesizing is commonly associated with higher-order critical thinking (Bloom, 1956), as it involves the refining of information to move to a solution, but synthesis importantly happens both during reading and post reading, and can form part of a self-monitoring process. Furthermore, in Ward et al.'s (1999) work on the generative process of creative thinking, synthesis is the springboard for the transformation of an idea into something new, so it can be regarded as both simultaneously convergent, a bringing together of ideas, and divergent, a springboard for creative thinking.

Taking the research literature around transactional strategies for comprehension as a starting point, the approaches the children in the study seemed to take in their tackling of the task of making meaning can be broadly categorized into four themes:

1. Determining importance and making connections to existing knowledge;
2. Asking questions and making predictions (or hypothesizing) to find out more;
3. Creating narratives and evoking images to extend and explain the story-world;
4. Empathizing with characters and entering the story-world to understand it more.

Determining importance and making connections to existing knowledge

The starting point for all of the vignettes is the decision to concentrate on a particular aspect of the text (whether visual or written), and as previously suggested, this setting of the task can be seen as a largely critical-thinking move. It could be argued that this is more directed in some of the texts than in others. For example, the centralized figure in *The Lady of Shalott* could reasonably be said to command more attention than her surrounding regalia, though not to Harry and Ben, who concentrate on the features around her. Within the narrative structure of *Way Home* the central character is Shane, and it is not surprising if the children concentrate on his motivations. However, the point here is that the dialogic readers agree (or not) to concentrate on a particular part of the text that opens the possibility of discussion and enables creative and critical thinking. Two children who have not yet featured in this book are Bella and Georgia, Year 1 (Y1) children who talk together to make sense of *They're Biting* (Klee, 1920). The painting represents semi-abstract figures who appear to be fishing. The shapes are line-drawn and include abstract symbols in addition to more recognizable shapes. In the centre of the work is what appears to be an exclamation mark. Much of their conversation is, as Mercer (2000) would term, 'disputational' and their discussion will be highlighted in Chapter 7. However, they provide an interesting example of how, even in disagreement, their first action is to identify a central point for focus.

01	*Bella*	Well
02	*Georgia*	We've got a man and it . . . it . . .
03	*Bella*	Well there's a woman and it looks like that's curly hair and she's facing *that way* [*speaker's emphasis*]
04	*Georgia*	Yeah, anyway, and it looks like that man is actually putting that in the water

The children try to make sense of shapes that look familiar and seem to be figures. Their point of disagreement is that Georgia thinks that the main figure is a man, and Bella decides it is a woman. They each ignore the suggestions of the other, as they determine the importance of the text features themselves. The extract offers a stark contrast to the approach of Harry and Ben, with Harry's invitation 'Right, what do you think it is first?' when discussing *The Lady of Shalott* as the boys are actively working together, even if directed explicitly by Harry. It is interesting to compare the boys' opening comments about *Golconde*, however:

M01	*Ben*	A kind of a film.
M02	*Harry*	Yeah, what film is it from? And are these people here, (*points*) are these men or ladies?
M03	*Ben*	Men. (*Both pause to look*) . . . They might be . . . (*looks at camera*)
M04	*Harry*	And . . . But are they womens? They might be black raindrops that look like womens, mightn't they?

While Ben makes the opening comment about the picture reminding him of a film, Harry does not make the same connection, and so quickly focuses on the figures instead. Similarly to Bella and Georgia, there is some disagreement about whether the figures are male or female, with the same approach taken by Harry to ignore Ben's suggestion that the figures might be men, as he has already determined the importance of them being female. This highlights a potential issue for reading together as dialogic partners. If focusing attention, determining importance and accessing known schema are important parts of comprehension, this becomes difficult when two readers essentially have different knowledge and interests. They therefore need to negotiate to interpret the text together, and this might depend on who has the most forceful opinion. Ben seems happy to collude with Harry's suggestions, and adds to them. Bella and Georgia, however, are less inclined to compromise, so they both continue their individual lines of thinking, rather than inter-thinking.

Themes that are deemed important may recur through the discussion, brought to the fore by the reader who identified them as important. So, when looking at the discussion between Alex and Sam (see previous chapter for the transcript), while they both discuss the themes of cats and homelessness, it is Sam who tends to initiate ideas about running away and being homeless, where Alex introduces the idea of cats. The difference for these two 11-year-old dialogic readers is that they collaborate more fully, and are able to weave both themes together. It is difficult to claim that this ability derives from their greater experience as older children, as the data set for the study is so small; suffice to say that it is possible for primary-aged children to engage collaboratively in this manner, drawing on quite sophisticated skills of synthesis and negotiation with no direct adult intervention.

From a sociocultural perspective, it is clear that cultural influences will impact on the children's interpretation of the text, while this may be problematic if there is not a 'match' between either text and readers (Palincsar and Brown, 1984) or between dialogic readers. This is perhaps shown through the examples above. However, shared cultural influences are also apparent in the children's discussions. In their discussion about *Golconde*, Harry and Ben discuss the possibility that the men are in the sky because of helicopters that have dropped them there. When challenged how one plane or helicopter could hold so many people, Ben gestures with his arms to create the image there could be 'one, one, one'. When Harry suggests there could be ten helicopters, Ben again repeats the same pattern, saying there could be 'another ten . . . and . . . another ten and another ten and another ten'. Both children have bought into an explanation that can be seen as a very plausible solution by drawing on their (potential) exposure to computer-gaming cartoon images – with the idea of a repetitious 'setting out' of the men in the sky. The difficulty with taking the sociocultural view is that the influences are not always explicit, and imposed on the interpretation of what Harry and Ben describe is an adult researcher perspective on what they might have experienced as 6-year-olds.

Sometimes, however, the cultural references to other texts are more obvious. When Sophie and Gina discuss *Golconde*, their shared existing knowledge of the world, including other texts, is highly apparent in their discussion and they make connections to what they already know:

01 Sophie   That's really actually quite strange.
02 Gina   Yeah . . . there's lots of men and they kind of [seem to be] . . .
03 Sophie   [Reminds me of] Mary Poppins . . .
04 Gina   Hmm, but a male version . . .
05 Sophie   . . . of Mary Poppins.
06 Gina   And houses . . .
07 Sophie   It's like and like they're like just falling down.

08 *Gina*   [mmm] Just falling from the sky . . .
09 *Sophie* [Like] it's quite . . .
10 *Gina*   It really is raining men . . . (*smiles*)
11 *Sophie* (*smiles*) yeah.

Within the space of ten turns of speech they include two separate shared references, the first initiated by Sophie and the second by Gina. Again, there is still
some disagreement over the gender of the figures, but the cultural references are
clear (also referred to in the previous chapter). The first is to *Mary Poppins*, a children's film (and book) of which the children must be aware and which includes a
nanny who can fly using her umbrella. Did I need to explain that, or might that
cultural reference be one shared with the readers of this text? The second is the
reference to *It's Raining Men*, a 1980s pop song. Interestingly, whenever I show
this picture to groups of adults, without fail someone mentions (smiling wryly) that
'it's raining men!' and laughs at the connection to the song; some even start to sing
it. Somehow the song has stood the test of time and embedded itself as a shared
cultural experience for these children.

The suggestion of shared cultural experience is also apparent with Harry and Ben,
and not just in the context of this study with them as 6-year-olds coming from similar
cultural backgrounds. An opportunity arose to work with the boys five years after the
initial research data were gathered and they were asked again to talk about *Rene Golconde* (Maine, 2014). They had no memory of the task as one they had undertaken in
Y1 and did not recognize the picture. They started the conversation thus:

01 *Harry* I think it looks quite weird.
02 *Ben*   Yeah it does.
03 *Harry* Quite a lot of men floating in the air . . . and they could be going up
         or down.
04 *Ben*   I think it's . . . it looks like it's raining . . . men
05 *Harry* Yeah (*laughs*) . . . quite a lot of men . . . They are all sort of dressed in
         the same thing aren't they?

There are two fascinating points to be made here. The first is that as an 11-year-
old, Harry repeats the same comment he made as a 6-year-old about the men
'going up or down'. Again, when the picture is shown to countless adults, that
comment is rarely made; most people assume the figures are falling, yet uniquely
Harry makes virtually the same point about the possibility they are rising five years
on. Second, while the reference about 'raining men' is outside their cultural experience as 6-year-olds, as 11-year-olds they make the same link as Sophie and Gina. Of
course, on a different day, with a different setting, these comments might not have
been made. All that can be said with any certainty is that in the co-construction of
meaning from text, dialogic readers engage with each other and with text, drawing
on what they know and making connections to themselves and other texts (including musical ones!) they have encountered.

Asking questions and making predictions (or hypothesizing) to find out more

Once an aspect of the text has been identified for focus, questions about it are then raised, in some cases simultaneously, and these open the space for creative thinking. The degree to which this happens in relation to the actual language markers and co-constructive moves made has been discussed in the previous chapters, but the affordance of question-raising as a comprehension strategy is clear. The dialogic readers are not asking questions that can be directly answered by a literal observation of the text itself; they are asking questions beyond it, leading towards an understanding of causality or motivation. Of course, it must not be forgotten that the task brief was to 'ask questions and find out what the text is about'. However, it is interesting to look closely at these questions, to explore how successful they are in generating ideas and supporting co-constructed meaning, particularly when focusing on the questions raised in the Y1 pairings. For example, Liam and James only raise one question directly about the text, and it is the starting point of the discussion (transcript in Chapter 4). James asks why the chameleons attacked the lizard in *Otherwise*, although in fact the discussion then turns to a descriptive re-telling of the story and it emerges that James knows the answer to the question he has asked. Not only that, he also often includes 'I know why . . . ' in his contribution, a phrase that Liam also picks up. For these two Y1 children, the tone of their talk is less exploratory and more confirmatory. Their lack of genuine questioning limits their ability to look beyond the literal in the text. This may of course be due to the text that they have discussed, as it does have a strong narrative, though it is non-verbal and requires the inference of understanding that the lizards in the story do not like the chameleon because he is 'different'. The question raised by James shows that he is engaging with the underlying messages in the animated tale: that it is about friendship and inclusion, or exclusion. However, the question serves as a vehicle for a re-telling: it is a question that is checking what is already known, rather than a divergence into a dialogic meaning-making outside the frame of the text, or an extension of the text-world. Instructed to raise questions about the text, James has fulfilled the task, but his understanding of how questions can lead to exploration seems less secure. In a similar way, Bella and Georgia ask more questions when discussing *They're Biting*, but these do not steer their comprehension of the text. Perhaps the text is too ambiguous and abstract, the complete opposite of *Otherwise*, so they are struggling to connect it to anything that they know at all. When all of their questions are analyzed together, it can be argued that they are more 'demands' for knowledge than divergent affordances:

07 *Bella*   Which fish . . . which part of the picture do you think is really neat?
10 *Bella*   Yeah and like why is it like an invisible thing?
11 *Georgia*   And why is that question mark there . . . ?
14 *Bella*   Why's that on it?
17 *Georgia*   Why is that there? Yeah and why?

Again their emphasis is on the question 'why', though they do not assume to know the answers, as James does in the example above. On the other hand, Hannah and Anna raise a number of questions that do lead them towards making meaning from their text, and they demonstrate that the use of 'why' in questions can launch a genuine creative line of enquiry, as illustrated by the extract below:

03	*Hannah*	While she's sailing on the boat . . . Why's her skirt hanging out in the water?
04	*Anna*	I don't know, probably she just wants to get her skirt wet so she can dry it, so, cos she, look it's quite muddy isn't it? (*Points at screen*)
05	*Hannah*	Mm
06	*Anna*	It's quite muddy.
07	*Hannah*	Maybe it's muddy cos she [went] . . .
08	*Anna*	[Went] in the mud.
09	*Hannah*	Yeah then she needs like, like went on the boat and she like hanged it [over in the water] . . .
10	*Anna*	[Yeah, so, what]
11	*Hannah*	. . . to clean it all up.

The questions raised lead to suggestions, and generative thinking (Ward et al., 1999), a process that is also illustrated through the way that Harry and Ben use questions to generate possible meanings. When pondering the existence of the men in the sky in *Golconde*, their ideas are strung together through a series of questions: are the figures 'going up or down?' 'How are they getting up there?' 'How can an aeroplane or helicopter hold so many people?' For each question the boys generate an explanation, and problematize this by enquiring further until they are satisfied with their solution: 'I think that's about it we can think of', concludes Harry.

Being able to ask genuine, divergent questions leads to a dialogic interaction between the children and the text, and between the children themselves. Their questions lead them to predict, or hypothesize, meanings that are rationalized to ensure that they make sense. The positing of a suggestion or prediction can be regarded as a divergent step in creative joint problem-solving and one that forms an important part of the comprehension process. The questions that the dialogic readers ask illuminate the pivotal role that 'possibility thinking' (Craft, 2000) and the positing of ideas and suggestions take in the co-construction of meaning of visual texts.

Creating narratives and evoking images to extend and explain the story-world

The importance of narrative in understanding the world is well documented (Bruner, 1986; Wells, 2009). It is, after all, a 'primary act of mind' (Hardy, 1977) and a fundamental tool for making sense (see Chapter 2). It is not surprising, then, that the dialogic readers, in making sense of the visual texts they are presented with, turn to narrative to rationalize and explain them. Researchers who have defined different comprehension strategies talk broadly about the importance of image creation in sense-making (Pressley, 2006; Keene and Zimmerman, 1997). It is interesting that their theories relate to written (or verbal) text and only an evocation of image, yet when faced with visual texts the children create verbal stories and more visual imagery. They move beyond the frame of the text to contextualize what they are experiencing, and this is true for both the purely visual and the multi-modal text types they encounter.

Anderson and colleagues describe a possible response to text as 'rhetorical extensions to the story world' (2001), which is a useful metaphor to describe the narratives the children create to make sense of the texts. However, because not all of the texts have an implicit story, here the response to text is renamed 'extension of the text-world' and refers to moments when the children create stories or describe possible events that are situated outside the frame of the text. Of course, because this is a collaborative enterprise, the children create these images and narratives together, meaning that they need to not just create the image or narrative but also make it plausible to their talk partner. This is most evident in the creations of Harry and Ben, whose computer-gaming image of multiple helicopters and practical solutions of ladies using cats to catch fish are driven by Harry and 'bought into' by Ben, who provides rationalizations for the ideas and extends them further when they do not make sense. Anna and Hannah also move beyond the frame of *The Lady of Shalott* to explain why the figure might be sitting in a boat. Their narrative explanation is plausible, and reasonably drawn from their existing schema. People with muddy clothes might get told off and be sent to clean up, even possibly having to have their tea outside. The idea of constructing narratives moves beyond the suggestion of creating images and perhaps is a necessary extension for these models of comprehension to also include visual texts. Children whose text experience is heavily based in narratives might well be predisposed to create stories from modes of text with spatial pathways, creating causality and motivations to explain them.

While the examples above lean on the vignettes where the texts were purely visual, the children who experience more obviously narrative texts (either written or visual) in the main vignette data do still employ this as a strategy for meaning-making, even if they are extending the text-world by including prior events or conclusions. Here the 'frame' of the text becomes temporal – what happened before or after – and fits with a linear reading pathway. While re-telling the story of their text, Liam and James take a narrative leap with Liam's suggestion that at the end of the story the chameleons and lizard live together, and this is initially challenged by James as 'we didn't see that bit when they lived together'. They then finish their re-telling of the story with a classical story ending, this time negotiating that 'they all lived happily ever after'. While this is a formulaic response, they are still extending the story beyond what is seen in the text and predicting a plausible story ending. It is interesting that James challenges Liam's initial narrative extension yet is happy to provide the 'stock' ending for the re-telling.

Alex and Sam generate a number of possibilities for why Shane might be homeless in *Way Home*. These short narratives are jointly constructed and include a number of possibilities, yet importantly do exist beyond the text-world:

34	*Sam*	Yeah, reckon like one of the cats must have died and like he wanted to get another one?
35	*Alex*	Yep or the cat ran away.
36	*Sam*	I'm just wondering how, why, I'm wondering if he used to have a proper home or something?
37	*Alex*	Or he got thrown out cos his mum and dad, wasn't, yeah he like ran away from home and stuff.
38	*Sam*	Or he was an orphan?
39	*Alex*	Yeah.

The children are searching beyond the literal to make meaning and they are doing so by generating questions and possibilities. Within six short lines of dialogue they have covered three reasons why Shane might live in a cardboard den, and two reasons why he picked up the cat. They have determined the importance of the cat and the surprise about Shane's home as the central ideas in the text, and generate solutions around them.

An interesting feature of the co-constructive talk in Sophie and Gina's discussion is that they try to extend what it is possible to see in the text, as if the clues to meaning are somehow just out of sight. For Sophie it is the possibility of the landscape behind the houses:

21	*Sophie*	What if there's a lake?
22	*Gina*	And they might go falling into it . . .
23	*Sophie*	Yeah . . . it's like wonder what's over there . . .

Rather than seeking meanings by creating narratives, Sophie is constructing an extension of the text-world through creating an image, though it does little to support her understanding of the picture itself or help her generate plausible explanations.

Extending the world of the text uses the strategies of both inference and synthesis as defined by Keene and Zimmerman (1997). The children need to infer possibilities from the information presented to them, and also to synthesize all their existing knowledge. When Hannah and Anna decide that the Lady of Shalott has been banned from the house because of her dirty skirt, they are synthesizing their own prior knowledge of the world and bringing it to their co-construction. When Sophie and Gina make reference to the song *It's Raining Men*, they are drawing on the wider cultural context and their knowledge of the world. The creative comprehension strategies the children use are interwoven, and with the extra dimension of the reading as a social and dialogic event, the act of comprehending meaning from text becomes dynamic. The narratives the children create to explain the texts need to be acceptable to both contributors, and therefore they are negotiated and constructed jointly.

Empathizing with characters and entering the story-world to understand it more

The last significant theme in the children's text comprehension moves in almost the opposite direction from an extension of the text-world. In all the texts that feature a main character, the children empathize to some degree to explain the actions (or perceived actions) within the text. In both vignettes that feature the picture book *Way Home*, the children empathize with the characters to gain a greater understanding, and in fact place emphasis on the same part of the story, when Shane rescues a kitten from a tree and stows it inside his jacket. For Alex and Sam, this happens when discussing why the kitten Shane picks up does not merely run away:

15 *Alex*   I was a bit surprised the cat went into there, so quickly, without being really scared.
16 *Sam*   Yeah I know, you walk up to a cat and it just legs it.
17 *Alex*   Yeah, and he just walked up to it and it went straight into his jacket.
18 *Sam*   I don't think he . . . I thought it was going to be like, when you saw the picture of the dog.
19 *Alex*   (unclear)
20 *Sam*   Yeah . . . I thought he was going to be like really scared and run off (unclear, background noise)
21 *Alex*   And then I thought that cat wouldn't come back to him, but . . .
22 *Sam*   Yeah I think that.
23 *Alex*   It's weird . . . there it is (*points*) . . .
24 *Sam*   Yeah, I got a I think that I'd probably leg it as well.
25 *Alex*   yeah (*both smile*)

After the initial suggestion that the events are surprising and not what was predicted, the effect is the same. Rather than extending the text-world through creating an additional narrative, they are entering it, and imagining what it would be like to be there – empathizing, in fact, with the kitten. Similarly, Tilly and Kate engage with the same part of the story, following a similar line of enquiry but empathizing with Shane, placing themselves in the position of picking up a stray kitten:

24 *Tilly*   Cos you wouldn't, I personally wouldn't, if I didn't have a friends, I just wouldn't pick up a cat, you know, that's me, but . . .
25 *Kate*   Yeah cos you know anything could happen [yeah but] even if it is really sweet [but anything . . .]

Both sets of children have connected with the sense of danger in the particular episode, though they have taken different stances. Both examples include explicitly empathizing comments, indicated by the use of first person, but arguably at any point when the children project motivations for action or emotional responses onto the characters in a text, they are implicitly empathizing, or employing a 'theory of mind'.

Nikolajeva (2014) argues that the two dispositions are quite different. For her, theory of mind is an understanding of how others think, while empathy is more specifically related to how others feel. While this is a valid separation, here the importance is that to do either of these things, the dialogic reader must step into the text, to see it from the inside. Therefore, the moments when Anna and Hannah decide that the Lady of Shalott has to eat her tea on the boat, and James' assertion that 'the brown one didn't want to get killed', can be called 'theory of mind' strategies where to understand the text, the children enter the text-world through the eyes of a character. The use of empathy/theory of mind as a comprehension strategy is identified by Lewis and Tregenza (2007), although viewing it as a linked strategy to the evocation of images (Keene and Zimmerman, 1997) or to the extension of the text-world is not a connection made by these authors. In this study, these two strategies (entering or extending the story-world) can be seen as paramount in the deepening and widening meanings in the dialogic space of possibility as they afford an enhanced perspective on the text at hand. They take the children beyond literal interpretations of the text as they explore the feelings and motivations of characters.

Children may extend or enter the text-world by creating narratives outside the frame of the text or by empathizing with a main character, or seeing the world through their eyes with a 'theory of mind'. They do this by determining the importance of text features, making inferences and synthesizing information within the text and from their own world knowledge. This critical-thinking, 'problem-solving' approach to making meaning from the text leads the children to rationalize and explain their perspectives. In fact, these explanations are often creative narratives themselves; for example, the reasons given by Alex and Sam for the rescue of the cat, or the reasons given by Hannah and Anna for why the Lady of Shalott's dress is muddy. In this way, the use of rationalizing and explaining demonstrates the dualistic nature of critical and creative thinking and how they represent the two sides of the 'special kind of problem-solving' coin defined by Nickerson (1999: 394). It is the fluency with which the children alternate between strategies that indicates the complexity and subtlety of the dialogic, critical and creative processes involved. The comprehension strategies the children use are closely tied to the affordances of the metaphorical dialogic space of possibility, as they enable the co-construction of meaning to follow different lines of enquiry based on the negotiation of provisional meanings. In particular, the creation of narratives beyond the frame of the text and empathy with characters within the text serve to further the discussion.

Returning to the idea of a dialogic space between text and reader, the data are used to illustrate how readers widen and deepen this metaphorical space by entering the world of the text – either to extend the story-world and create narratives to explain it, or to deepen the space through empathizing with characters or placing themselves in the 'scene' to engage with it. The approach the dialogic readers take is similar in both verbal and visual texts. These 'entanglement' (Iser, 1978) strategies are important as they allow the children to create meanings from a different standpoint rather than their own, and this approach is touched upon in the cognitive theories of reader response that draw on the importance of theory of mind. Crucially, all the children show that they can do this – the 6-year-olds as well as the 11-year-olds – as they draw on their existing schema to help them. Is it surprising that Harry and Ben construct gaming images, or that Liam and James interpret the 'friends' and 'inclusion' themes in their story? This extends beyond simply trying to see the world from the protagonist's point of view, and brings the world view of the reader as the lens through which to see. Protherough's (1983) study explores the positioning of child readers as they engage with (written) texts. He describes a continuum of distance and immersion in children's descriptions of their interaction with stories, which range from a detached evaluation of the story to a full immersion with the character in it. His argument is that in schools there is too much emphasis placed on evaluation and not enough on immersion. The refreshing consideration in this study, then, is that without direct adult engagement, the most frequently occurring position is within or beyond the text as children become entangled in it.

Chapter summary

This chapter began by considering the traits of different transactional or comprehension strategies to be indicative of critical or creative thinking, drawing on reading comprehension research that has been particularly prevalent since the turn of the century, albeit particularly relating to the 'instruction' of reading in North America. Using this literature as a framework, four main themes were explored through the children's discussion of visual texts that illustrated how they engaged with the text as dialogic readers: determining the importance of text features based on their own existing schema; asking questions and proposing hypotheses to think of possibilities; filling the gaps of meaning with their own narratives that extended beyond the text-world, either spatially or temporally; and making sense of the 'scene' through entering it and empathizing with characters. A connection was made to reader response and cognitive theories of children's reading, to balance the initial concentration on comprehension and instruction. The term 'meaning-making' is chosen as somewhere between 'comprehension' (which feels loaded with assumptions about instruction and teaching) and 'response' (which feels loaded with assumptions about the aesthetics of literature and art). The chapter began with a quotation from Benton (2004) and I return to it. Meaning is not discovered; it is created. Reading is dialogic when it enables a creation of meaning through a dialogic space of possibility, or as Smith (2010) describes, 'by importing the unread text into the projected imaginative space' of a reader's mind.

The next chapters turn our attention to the meta-level engagement the children show as they co-construct meaning from text, or as Barnes and Todd would describe, the 'interactive frame' (1995). Metacognitive awareness and self-monitoring are considered central tenets of reading comprehension and are highlighted in theories about critical and creative thinking. So, while there are overlaps with the other themes discussed in this chapter, the children's awareness of the process they are engaged in is explored explicitly in the next.

6

REFLECTING TOGETHER

The importance of self-monitoring and metacognition

The previous chapters have concentrated on the meaning being made by the dialogic readers and how their language indicates their thinking and comprehension – the content of the co-construction. These next two chapters now concentrate on how the children manage the interactive process, and how what they say shows their awareness of the task at hand and how they monitor their own progression with it. Barnes and Todd suggest that these two kinds of meaning represent two different 'frames' of interpretation: a *content frame* that 'offers an interpretation of the subject in hand', and an *interaction frame* that 'offers an interpretation of the social relationships which are shaping the interaction' (Barnes and Todd, 1995: 145). The interaction frame indicates the children's ongoing awareness of the process in which they are engaged, and illuminates the children's sense of their own thinking, their dialogue and the task and context in which the dialogic reading event is happening. It is indicated when they step outside the content of their co-construction, to make comments about their thinking, the process or the situation. This 'self-monitoring and reflexivity' (1995: 9) is an important indicator of creative and critical thinking, and includes 'metacognition' or thinking about thinking. Littleton and Mercer (2013: 101) use the term 'co-regulation' to highlight the joint nature of this endeavour when children are working and talking together, recognizing that the terms 'self'-monitoring or 'self'-regulation emphasize, of course, the individual. In this study, the children's language is analyzed to illuminate this 'awareness of process' and to explore the different levels on which it happens as they engage with the task. Sometimes this awareness relates to their own thinking, while at other times it reflects the co-constructive process. For this reason, the term 'co-regulation' has not been adopted, though consideration of the joint enterprise underpins all of the analysis. In the transcripts, the co-constructive moves that are deemed to reflect this 'awareness of process' are coded P-Process moves.

The role of reflection and metacognition in critical and creative thinking

Highlighted in the definitions of both critical and creative-thinking processes is the concept of metacognition or 'knowledge and cognition about cognitive phenomena' (Flavell, 1979: 906). Several writers (for example, Lipman, 2003; Ennis, 1987) identify self-correcting or reflection and self-monitoring as key features of critical and creative thinking. These can be identified as metacognitive, with the thinker turning their thoughts inwards onto their own thought processes. In their comprehensive guide to different theoretical frameworks for thinking, Moseley et al. (2005) describe the difference in approach that philosophers and psychologists take to defining critical and creative thinking. They argue that philosophers take a more 'normative' approach, looking at thinking as a whole, and making judgements about value and quality. For example, Robinson in his definition of creativity (2001) describes the importance of making judgements about creative work (in this case, thinking). Earlier, in the oft-quoted National Advisory Committee on Creative and Cultural Education (NACCCE) document, creativity is defined as 'imaginative activity fashioned so as to produce outcomes that are both original and of value' (1999: 29). The thinker or creator is implicitly involved in making ongoing judgements about the quality of their creative thought. On the other hand, psychologists, argue Moseley et al., are more inclined to examine processes and their approaches can be defined as more 'descriptive' (2005: 19). Nickerson et al. (1985), for example, discuss the role of metacognition more thoroughly. First, they discuss the 'expert' problem-solver who 'works on solving the problem, and watches himself critically as he does so' (1985: 9). They go on to discuss different aspects of metacognition; 'effective planning and strategizing' and 'monitoring and evaluation of one's knowledge and performance' (1985: 114). The thinker is conscious of his or her starting point and goals, and is therefore able to plan according to the whole task, rather than let it unfold in front of them. Fundamentally, this reflective mode is ongoing, and successful thinkers and solution-finders are able to monitor, adjust and realign their thinking. Whereas other writers imply a judicious awareness and modification of ideas as integral to metacognition, the two aspects identified by Nickerson et al. suggest a movement between *in-process* reflection and *on-process* reflection; that is, reflection that is fluid and running concurrently with the critical and creative thought processes in action, while also including strategic planning and retrospective reflection outside the process.

To link back to Chapter 2 and Hymes' (1972) model of speech acts, events and situations, this metacognitive dimension relates specifically to the overarching context of the 'event' that the participants are aware they are engaged in. If the problem or task is viewed as the 'event', then the monitoring and metacognitive strategies that assist successful outcomes not only situate the participants but show their active engagement with it. When metacognition, which is implied as a sophisticated critical-thinking skill, is exemplified as such, then the complexity of the processes that the dialogic readers are engaged in becomes very apparent.

Not only are they exploring ideas through both problem-finding and solution-finding, but to negotiate this process successfully they are reflecting both 'in' and 'on' the process itself, and engaged ultimately in a complex and sophisticated inter-dimensional cognitive process.

The role of reflection and self-monitoring in reading

The previous chapter explored the theories around reading comprehension and the teaching of transactional strategies to support meaning-making from text. Self-monitoring or metacognition is regarded as central to reading comprehension along with seeking clarification when elements of text are misunderstood (Keene and Zimmerman, 1997; Palincsar and Brown, 1984; Pressley, 2000, 2006). It is the self-checking element that runs parallel to the meaning-making event. Drawing on her original work with Brown (1984), Palincsar (2003) advocates a teaching approach designed to enable readers to 'self-regulate', with the explicit modelling of strategies that centre on this awareness of one's own reading process. Even her definition of 'strategies' centralizes self-awareness, as she describes them as planful approaches that learners bring to organizing and monitoring their activities as readers' (Palincsar, 2003: 100). Comprehension and self-monitoring are then synonymously linked for successful readers, and therefore further aligned with the wider theories of critical and creative thinking.

The monitoring of understanding is important regardless of text form, though (as in the case of 'prediction' highlighted in the last chapter) there are issues if the text is simultaneously present, as in a picture. In a linear text, the intended meaning gradually emerges, and while readers might make their own interpretations and responses, they can check the hypotheses of their meaning-making as the text progresses. Features of a picture might carry clues to meaning, but hypotheses cannot be tested in the same way. It is at this point that the act of co-construction becomes important as the children can monitor and reflect on their joint understanding, challenging and rationalizing ideas together. Littleton and Mercer (2013) argue that this 'co-regulation' acts as a model for future intra-mental thinking, while Paul (1987) would argue that it paves the way for dialogical thinking, and the ability to reason and provide counter-arguments with oneself.

In the vignettes, the comments the children make that show their awareness and regulation of the task can be organized into two themes: their awareness and regulation of the thinking processes they are engaged in (that is, their metacognition and their judgements about their thinking), and their awareness and regulation of the task they are involved in, including their management of it at the start, during and end of their discussion. Ordered in this way, the themes start with the central notion of the children's thinking and move out through Hymes' 'nested hierarchy' of co-constructive act, event and situation (Rojas-Drummond et al., 2006). A detailed analysis of the readers' social enterprise is considered in the next chapter and so moments where they show themselves to be monitoring their social action will be considered there.

Awareness and regulation of own thinking

The pairs of children are all aware of the task they have been set and the goals of that task. They are used to asking questions and talking together, and know that the teacher-researcher values the discussion, not just the outcome. This is important because it means that the children are not focused on an end point, but rather on raising questions and talking about the visual texts. This type of exploratory task sets up both a value and process focus, and while the children do not make many comments about their thinking, the comments do illustrate an awareness and judgement, or evaluation of their approach. In Harry and Ben's two discussions, they both make comments about their thinking and the quality of it. In the discussion about the Magritte painting (transcript in Chapter 3), when Harry declares (line 14) 'I wonder if they are going up or down', he quickly follows it with 'That's a question isn't it?' In the video data, he clearly places emphasis on 'that's' rather than 'question', the tone indicating that there is a missing adjective – the emphasis is not on the fact that he has asked a question and recognizes it as such, but rather that it is a 'good' question. Similarly, when discussing *The Lady of Shalott* and in particular the type of waterway that the painting might depict, in response to Harry's question (line 15), 'Is it on the river or is it on the sea?', Ben declares, 'Now that's a good question. Now I don't know that one.' The children are clearly focused on the task of asking valuable questions that will help them find out what the picture is 'all about'. They may only make two such comments, but this is a concentration on the interaction frame, not the content frame; their main focus is finding a solution to the texts' meaning, and their comments about the process are reminders that this is a task and they have a goal. As the children move through their discussion, they are monitoring their performance against the task set, showing their ability to remain focused and goal-orientated. What is interesting about this is the particular context of the thinking task. They are in an educational setting, and it is an educational task. The motivation is to successfully complete the task, and possibly to 'please the teacher' rather than to talk about the text purely for its own sake, and the comments above reflect this. They are implying qualitative judgements about their approach to the task, a quality that is reflected in definitions of creativity and creative thinking (for example, NACCCE, 1999; Robinson, 2001); they are evaluating the quality of their questions and deciding that they are good ones.

There are two further instances of comments that demonstrate Harry and Ben's reflection on the process of their thinking, which happen within their discussion of the Waterhouse painting (transcript in Chapter 3), and these show more subtle awareness of self-monitoring. The first is from Ben (line 08) when he says, 'Yeah that's what's I was just about to say!'

Although almost just a turn of phrase, Ben seems to indicate awareness of his own thought process. Later, Harry (line 43) explicitly judges his ability to fulfil the task based on his experiences outside the classroom, 'Yeah that would be kind of wouldn't it? That would fit. I'm quite good at doing all these because, umm, I'm in a school that goes around solving mysteries. It's called the Pig Snout.'

These examples of the children's reflection 'in' and 'on' the process of their co-construction make apparent the complexity of the thinking processes in which they are engaged. The examples also strengthen the argument that the critical and creative inter-thinking of these young children demonstrates a complex and sophisticated set of strategies. The way that children show awareness of the process of the reading event varies, from a self-monitoring of the quality of their thinking to a focus on the task itself. Following Moseley et al.'s (2005) description, this difference can be defined as more critical (the self-monitoring or strategic planning of the process of engagement) or creative (concerned with the quality of thinking).

Based on the coding and frequency of P-Process comments, the most reflective dialogue occurs between Alex and Sam in their discussion of the picturebook *Way Home* (transcript in Chapter 4). This is interesting because *Way Home* has a clear, linear narrative structure, and the children engage with the whole text before discussing it. However, these children do not simply retell the narrative; they make comments (in particular, Alex) about their reactions to it. Below is the start of their discussion and the first dialogic chain of thinking (that is, all of the comments related to one idea, before a new line of thinking is initiated, and marked as **DCT**):

01 Alex **DCT1** That was nothing like I thought it was gonna to be . . . I thought it was gonna like go to a building or something but . . . mmm . . . just went to a cardboard box.
02 Sam   I thought like he was going like to go to like a really nice house or something like that.
03 Alex But then when it got into the middle part, it um like got nearer towards the junk stuff I thought that's turning into . . . er . . . (*pause*) and **DCT2** I think his whole life is devoted to cats.

Because the discussion is retrospective, the children reflect on their process of reading, but rather than just describing what they think now that they have read it, they describe their thinking at particular points in the reading process. So Alex includes, 'I thought' and then projects himself back into that reading moment. His first turn in the discussion reflects on his response to the whole text. He recognizes that his thinking changed and that he did not accurately predict the ending of the book. From a 'normative' (Moseley et al., 2005) definition of creative thinking, he is judging his interpretation and how the book developed. Because his reflection is a review of his thinking, reflecting back on the whole process, it is a reflection 'after' the thinking has happened and is more summative. He goes on to describe the moment when his thinking changed, and how he began to change his prediction of the story's outcome. His position outside the content frame of the discussion is emphasized by his direct reporting of his past thinking (line 03), 'I thought, that's turning into . . . ', showing him to be reflecting 'on' his thinking. Sam also uses the term 'I thought' and uses it to extend the suggestion that Alex has just made, agreeing that his prediction was also that Shane would be going home to a nice house rather than a cardboard box. There is a marked difference in the use of 'I thought' in these three turns, from the use of 'I think . . . because' which is defined as an indicator of exploratory talk (Mercer, 2000). In fact, as the children are always describing what they thought about the text in this vignette, they often use the phrase. However, the example discussed above shows that the use of the phrase might have a subtly different reflective function, rather than an exploratory one, as the boys are open about the fact that their original assumptions about the text were incorrect.

Within Alex and Sam's discussion, the other comments that have been coded as P-Process include an indication of acknowledged 'surprise', and are listed below:

10 *Sam*   And, um, I'm just surprised.
15 *Alex*   I was a bit surprised that the cat went into there, so quickly, without being really scared.
29 *Alex*   I'm surprised actually.

As with the examples of Alex's use of 'I thought' in the first lines of dialogue, the use of the word 'surprise' and its function within the turns shows a reflective element to the thinking. The children are acknowledging their changes in thinking, monitoring their success in predicting the outcome of the story, and reflecting on their mismatch of expectations from the story's outcome.

Awareness and regulation of the task

From the perspective of Nickerson et al. (1985), central to the process of critical thinking is the strategic planning of thinking and the ongoing monitoring of it. As dialogic readers, the children have a task to engage with and they demonstrate an awareness of this through their comments to each other. They organize the task and use 'structuring moves' (Sinclair and Coulthard, 1975: 12) to engage in it. A good example of this type of move is undertaken by Harry at the beginning of the discussion about *The Lady of Shalott*, when he starts with, 'Right what do you think it is first?' This initial comment demonstrates a strategic approach, both in the initial word 'right', which signifies a definite starting point, and 'first', which shows that he has decided that this is the appropriate order.

The children's talk is not 'context free' and the roles that they take reflect the communicative situation in which it is located. In this case, it is interesting to note that in the absence of a teacher during the discussion, Harry takes on the role of task organizer by asking questions about the text. However, while assuming the leading role, he is equally searching for a solution, so the questions take the enquiry forward, rather than checking the understanding of Ben. Therefore, to make a structuring move like the one above suggests a 'directing stance' assumed by Harry, as he has taken charge of the direction of the discussion, deciding that the priority is to decide what they are looking at. This is different to the 'teacherly stance' described in Chapter 5 which happens when one of the children assumes the role of the teacher and 'tests' the other child. Here the function of the position remains co-constructive: Harry is simply taking charge of the joint enterprise. He is aware of the task at hand and is prioritizing the feature of text that he feels is the key to its successful interpretation.

Similarly, the final comment from Harry and glance to the camera from Ben when talking about *Golconde* are strategic and act as structuring moves. Satisfied with the story about helicopters and planes, Harry declares, 'I think that's about it we can think of' (M26). Ben responds by looking directly at the camera, a clear awareness that not only have they been engaged in a task, but that now it has been completed, the video can be switched off. A curious consideration might be that while a teacher is not physically present, their tool (the video camera) is, and so by implication they are still framing the discussion, which of course takes place in a classroom, in an educational setting. Ben's glance to the camera can be seen as 'to the teacher', and overtly aware of the co-constructive event.

There are points in the vignettes that demonstrate a more awkward awareness of the task, and perhaps an over-orientation towards the goal or outcome, rather than the quality of thinking. For Liam and James this occurs in the middle of their discussion, when the ideas stall. 'What do you want to say?' (line 19) whispers James, assuming a directing stance. That he whispers this comment is significant as it emphasizes that he knows this is not part of the discussion about the text, but a task-driven comment. It could also be seen to signify a slight embarrassment at being 'caught on camera' (again, the tool of the teacher having a presence).

At the end of the vignette James again assumes a directing stance by asking Liam if he has finished everything he wants to say. When Liam responds, the exchange takes on a much lighter tone, a relief that the task is done, perhaps. Liam repeats James' request and they both agree to finish the discussion:

31	James	. . . the other three went away to go back to their home and the other one, he wanted to live with them and it all lived happily ever after
32	Liam	(*smiles and eye contact, nods*) yeah
33	James	Finished?
34	Liam	Yeah, are you finished?
35	James	Yeah. Okay!

It is clear for both boys that the discussion is finished because they have rounded it off with an ending, 'happily ever after'. These two children seem to find the discussion difficult and never quite shake off their over-awareness of the task. Even all of James' 'I know why . . . ' comments, discussed in Chapter 4, can be seen as continual reminders that they are engaged in a task that James wants to get 'right', when the other children are happier to explore and play with ideas. The reasons for this are unclear. It may be that the text did not offer the children enough scope to explore their ideas, or that they were not comfortable as a pairing – or just that they were too overwhelmed by the task and the recording to engage in it in the same way as the others; but this does raise a question about process and goals, and how these are shared. The implications of considering talk, reading and thinking through a dialogic lens will be considered in the final chapter.

In another case where the awareness of the task is highly evident, Tilly and Kate discuss *Way Home*. All of the comments in their discussion that are coded with P-Process are included below:

20 *Tilly* All these questions were like popping into my head.
30 *Tilly* All these questions popping into my head.
58 *Tilly* There are questions, but then you find an answer, you find something else, and you think . . .
72 *Tilly* It just brings questions, loads and loads of questions

The first thing to notice about these coded comments is that all of them belong to Tilly. They are also essentially saying the same thing, that the text, *Way Home*, provokes lots of questions. However, within the discussion the children do not explore 'lots and lots of questions', focusing instead on the quality of the pictures, and the issues of why Shane picks up the cat and why his home is a cardboard den. As discussed in Chapter 4, the children in this vignette seem overly conscious of their task performance. They have been asked to raise questions to find out what the text is about, but are unable to explore it in any depth even though their discussion is significantly longer than all of the other discussions, most of which are transcribed in their entirety in this book. The open-ended prompts given did not support these children to have an exploratory discussion about the possibilities of meaning; but conscious of the task set, Tilly stays focused and instead comments on the process of her engagement as a means of successfully completing the task for the teacher.

The examples from the children's discussions shown above demonstrate that while an awareness of the task and its goals allows for strategic planning and summative reflection, an over-awareness of the task can lead to an awkwardness that inhibits creative thinking and leads the children to be goal-orientated (with the goal being to complete the task).

Chapter summary

This chapter has looked in detail at the first dimension of the *interaction* frame: the elements of the children's talk that reflect their awareness of the co-constructive event they are involved in. There are two levels of awareness of process that the children show as they engage in the task of making meaning from visual text: an awareness of their own thinking, and judgements about its quality; and an awareness of the task itself and how they are progressing with it. Having explored how the children are able to manage their thinking and the process of the task, our attention turns in the next chapter to how they manage each other and the joint enterprise of being dialogic readers.

7

LEARNING TOGETHER

Social cohesion as the foundation for co-constructive talk

The previous chapter explored the metacognitive awareness that the children in the study demonstrate as they reflect on their thinking, the task and the situation in which their discussions are taking place. This chapter forms a final analysis of the data considering how the children socially manage their discussion. This means looking closely at the social element of the dialogic readers' engagement with each other, and considering how they manage the talking, thinking, reading and reflecting, *together*. The goals of the task that the children are engaged in can be seen to be twofold. At one level there is the explicit meaning-making scenario, to ask questions and find out what the text is 'all about'. This goal is explicit and the rules are clear for the talk event, particularly because of the common understanding that the children have about this talk happening 'in school'.[1]

However, a second more implicit goal is apparent in the discussion, a social goal of harmony or *cohesion*. Without being explicitly directed by the teacher, the children know (and in most cases seem to desire) that they should negotiate with each other and end the discussion without having fallen out with each other. They are involved in co-constructive paired discussions, and this social context surrounds the co-constructive events and acts within it and affects the dialogic process. Therefore, running parallel with the creative and critical construction of meaning is an interwoven social dimension geared towards cohesion and as such enabling provisional meaning-making. The social interaction itself occurs within a specific cultural context, informing the children's approach to the task, and the unique prior knowledge that they bring to it.

This is also an appropriate point to reconsider Mercer's three modes of talk between peers: exploratory, cumulative and disputational talk (Mercer et al., 1999;

Mercer, 2000). For Mercer, only exploratory talk truly pushes learning forward, as a cumulative mode where children merely agree with each other and a disputational mode where they are working against each other add little value in the social mode. However, underpinning exploratory talk is the prerequisite that this can only happen if there is a degree of social cohesion, otherwise the talk would become disputational and not achieve its exploratory goals. Therefore, it could be argued that there *is* a place for cumulative talk action, where speakers are concerned with 'getting along', as it provides the bedrock on which more exploratory, creative co-construction can take place.

The foundation of social cohesion is even more important if the children are to engage in a discussion in which they may hold contrasting views, and still work to co-construct meaning. This concept is embedded in the broader 'over-arching framework of co-constructive talk' defined by Rojas-Drummond et al. (2006: 92). As discussed in Chapter 2, in this definition, negotiation and turn-taking mean that the speakers are committed to working together, and this prerequisite is the foundation on which potential, possible and provisional understandings can be built. The model of co-constructive talk proposed in Chapter 3 can therefore be extended to also include the social and cultural context surrounding the talk itself (see Figure 7.1).

There are several features of the children's discussions in this study that show how even the younger children quite skilfully negotiate these two goals and weave them together. There are also some examples of how this cannot be assumed, when children are either working so much at odds with each other or that they are so caught up in the desire to 'get on with each other' that the creative co-construction of meaning is compromised. These will be explored later in the chapter. Within the children's talk there are four themes that highlight the social goal of their talk and their ability to manage (or not manage) the discussion as a joint enterprise.

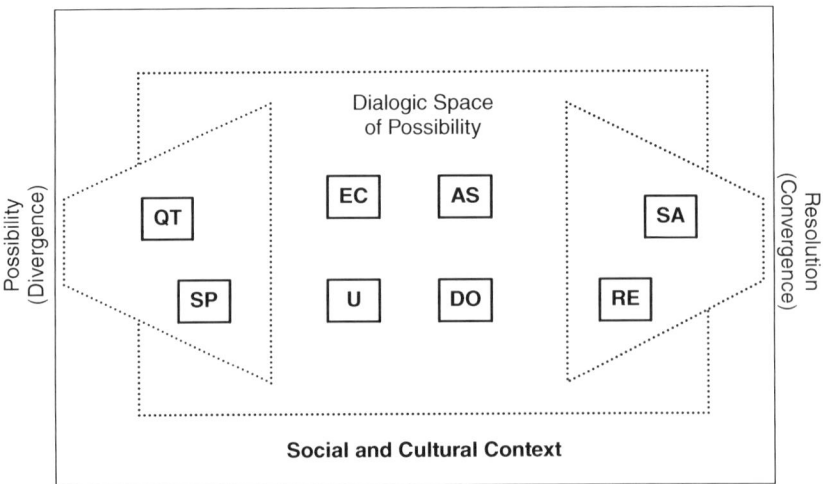

FIGURE 7.1 A model of co-constructive talk with social and cultural context

These themes draw on the literature and theory around talk that was explored in Chapter 2 and illustrate it by analyzing the vignettes. The first theme explores provisionality and the use of ambiguous and hypothetical language, this time as a means of maintaining a social cohesion that allows the task to be undertaken, rather than as a springboard for creative thinking. The second theme explores the use of connective words and phrases to build cohesion with previous turns and link the talk together, drawing on Wells' (1981) syntagmatic dimension. The third theme analyzes the way that the children use language creatively to build social cohesion and an 'affective convergence' (Carter, 2004). Finally, the fourth theme considers the cases where the children are either not socially cohesive, or where their focus seems to be so much on the 'getting along' that they fall into a cumulative discussion that limits their creative response.

Provisionality and the use of ambiguous, hypothetical language

In Chapter 2, the concept of *provisionality* was first raised as a point between speakers where meanings are ambiguous and rely on the listener as well as the speaker to make sense. In her work exploring children's informal language in the playground, Maybin (1994) argues that meanings are frequently contested and are dependent on the respondent as well as the speaker's intended meaning. She argues that the cognitive and social aspects of talk are closely interwoven and that even 'one utterance can (and usually does) serve a number of different cognitive and social purposes simultaneously' (1994: 148). Chapter 3 examined language indicators that demonstrate where a provisionality or 'hypothetical modality' (Barnes and Todd, 1995: 145) exist in the children's talk, highlighting words such as 'maybe', 'perhaps' and 'possibly'. However, if we include the potential of a social goal that motivates collaboration rather than just a meaning/clarity-seeking purpose, this would also explain the 'hypothetical modality' to be aimed at social cohesion rather than dissonance. In this case, the term 'hypothetical' might be better termed as 'potential' or 'possible', which would more precisely reflect the intention of keeping meaning provisional and open to negotiation as opposed to the set promotion of a theory. So, to return to Harry and Ben's discussion about Magritte, their provisionality is apparent in almost every turn (underlined) through their hypothetical language in the extract below:

M14	Harry	But . . . I wonder <u>if</u> they are going up or down. That's a question isn't it?
M15	Ben	[Hmm].
M16	Harry	Because they're going down on . . . They look like . . .
M17	Ben	[Cos cos they're on the floor]
M18	Harry	I know, but <u>they might</u> have been taking off . . . and how are they getting up there?
M19	Ben	[Yeah . . . or . . .] or <u>they might</u> have jumped out of a helicopter.
M20	Harry	I know. How can an aeroplane or a helicopter hold so many people in it?

M21	*Ben*	Well, there <u>could be</u> one, one, one, one (*gestures*) . . . it <u>could be</u> like . . .
M22	*Harry*	[There <u>could be</u> ten of them]
M23	*Ben*	And then they'd set out of another ten . . . and . . . another ten and another ten and another ten.
M24	*Harry*	[And] then they <u>might</u> all fly back up again and they <u>might</u> go and land somewhere else, <u>mighten</u> they?
M25	*Ben*	Yeah . . . and do something . . .

By offering possibilities rather than assumed facts, in theory Harry and Ben are allowing each other to offer alternatives or make their own contribution to the existing idea. Additionally, Harry also adds four questions that can be seen as invitations to Ben to contribute (M14, M18, M20, M24) or to agree with his ideas. Although Harry often takes the lead in discussions, in this extract their co-construction is more balanced, as Ben picks up the idea of helicopters and is keen to justify the suggestion.

If Anna and Hannah's discussion is analyzed in the same way, a similar pattern of hypothetical language and questioning is apparent:

01	*Hannah*	I think she's just <u>probably</u> sitting on a boat on . . . water?
02	*Anna*	I think she kinda wants to see like loads of pretty things, <u>isn't she</u>?
03	*Hannah*	While she's sailing on the boat . . . Why's her skirt hanging out in the water?
04	*Anna*	I don't know, <u>probably</u> she just wants to get her skirt wet so she can dry it, so, cos she, look it's quite muddy <u>isn't it</u>? (*Points at screen*)
05	*Hannah*	Mm
06	*Anna*	It's quite muddy.

The first line of speech is marked as a question because it finishes with a rising inflection, a tone that adds a provisionality to a statement, and this is followed by three further question turns, which include exploratory questions, 'Why's her skirt hanging out in the water?' (03) in addition to questions that seem to seek agreement: 'isn't she?', 'isn't it?' Even the response to the exploratory question has the caveat of 'probably' attached to it. The language of possibility was discussed at length in Chapters 3 and 4 in relation to creative thinking, but creative co-construction can only occur if the speakers have a social harmony or cohesion – something even these Year 1 (Y1) children achieve through using tentative words and phrases and seeking affirmation for their ideas from each other.

Using connective words and phrases to build cohesion

Another feature of the social dimension of this talk, also apparent in the two examples above, is the cohesion of the links between turns. Earlier, the notion of Wells' (1981) paradigmatic talk dimension was discussed, with little discussion of the other dimension he identifies, the syntagmatic, which looks at the connection between each link in the chain. Here our attention is turned to this latter dimension.

In addition to the provisional language and affirmation-seeking questions high-lighted above, the foundation of social cohesion is also reinforced by the connecting words and phrases that start each turn. To look again at the same section of talk from Harry and Ben:

M14	Harry	*But* . . . I wonder if they are going up or down. That's a question isn't it?
M15	Ben	[Hmm].
M16	Harry	*Because* they're going down on . . . They look like . . .
M17	Ben	[*Cos cos* they're on the floor]
M18	Harry	<u>I know,</u> *but* they might have been taking off . . . *and* how are they getting up there?
M19	Ben	[<u>Yeah</u> . . . *or* . . .] *or* they might have jumped out of a helicopter.
M20	Harry	<u>I know</u>. How can an aeroplane *or* a helicopter hold so many people in it?
M21	Ben	Well, there could be one, one, one, one (*gestures*) . . . it could be like . . .
M22	Harry	[There could be ten of them]
M23	Ben	*And* then they'd set out of another ten . . . *and* . . . another ten *and* another ten *and* another ten.
M24	Harry	[*And*] then they might all fly back up again *and* they might go *and* land somewhere else, mighten they?
M25	Ben	<u>Yeah</u> . . . *and* do something . . .

In the extract above, the conjunctions are marked in italics and the affirmations are underlined. Initially the conjunctions are problematizing and rationalizing: 'but' and 'because'. However, as the children develop their story and collaborate in its construction, they string together their ideas simply using 'and'. There are only two lines of speech that start with neither an affirmation nor a connective. One of these is line M15 which can be viewed as a 'repair' or 'hedging' statement (Fairclough, 1992), a word used to bridge between comments, generate space for thinking and maintain the dialogue. In the coding scheme (see Chapter 3) these are given the code U-Uncertainty, as they might indicate a lack of direction or non-commitment in the speech turn. The other turn (line M22) is a section of overlapped speech and shows Harry finishing Ben's sentence – which Ben then continues in the next turn of speech. This also happens between Anna and Hannah when they finish each other's sentences:

07	Hannah	<u>Maybe</u> it's muddy cos she [went] . . .
08	Anna	[Went] in the mud.

And continue each other's ideas:

27	Anna	Um, it's kind of, I think she's not allowed in the house cos she's so muddy . . .

28	*Hannah*	Yeah, so she had to go and wash herself.
29	*Anna*	. . . and she has to have tea on the boat.
30	*Hannah*	Tea on the boat! (*laughs*)

Hannah repeats the end of Anna's sentence and laughs, showing a cohesion and agreement about the end of the idea. The act of finishing off an idea for someone shows that you truly are in tune with what they are saying, and have reached an 'inter-subjective understanding' (Vygotsky, 1962: 237) where thinking is aligned. Of course, this can be highly irritating if the respondent moves the thinking into a different direction, unintended by the initiator, but this is not evident in the two examples above as the children are happy to continue to build the sentence over a number of turns. The children build cohesion in several different ways in the examples above and as a result are enabled to think and respond together.

Using language creatively to build social cohesion

The third theme of social cohesion in the children's talk is apparent in the way that they use language creatively to share understanding and work together. Sometimes this means explicitly making jokes or laughing together, but there are more subtle creative language uses that bring the speakers together. Tannen's (1989) research highlights different involvement strategies that are used by participants in a discourse who have an ultimate goal of coherence, and she particularly draws on the use of repetition in dialogue. She argues that 'repetition is a resource by which conversationalists together create a discourse, a relationship and a world. It is the central linguistic meaning-making strategy, a limitless resource for individual creativity and interpersonal involvement' (1989: 97). Taylor (2012) also describes the cohesive device of repeating, and how these repetitions can occur diachronically (that is, across time) or synchronically (through the echoing of words, for example in the last line of speech from Hannah, above).

Tannen identifies different facets of repetition in dialogue. Sometimes, she argues, repetition is used to create a cognitive space, where a speaker can remain fluent while formulating new ideas. It also provides a 'semantically less dense discourse' (1989: 97), aiding comprehension as ideas are processed. Repetition can provide a connection between ideas and speakers and this implies an underpinning flow and pattern of discourse that speakers 'invest in'. This could be merely defined as cumulative talk, but this would lead to an oversight on the nature of these repetitions, and how they demonstrate a playful creativity in the co-construction of meaning. For example, in each of their discussions, Harry and Ben make lists relating to buildings, boats and fish. Each turn of the dialogue adds a new item to the list, and in so doing, responds to the previous speech act. If this 'listing' is viewed as a repetitious linguistic feature, not through the use of the same words but through a repetition of concept, then the functions of repetition identified by Tannen remain applicable:

W03	*Harry*	And what kind . . . And what kind of boat is it? [Is it a motor boat?]
W04	*Ben*	[It's kind of a . . .] or is it a canoeing boat?
W05	*Harry*	Yeah, cos I can't see any oars on it, it must be an engine [boat].
W06	*Ben*	[Or . . .]
W07	*Harry*	It might not be a floating boat.
W08	*Ben*	[Or . . .] yeah that's what's I was just about to say.
W09	*both*	(*both laugh*)

As the boys list the different kinds of boats that might describe the one they see, they have given themselves a problem to solve, but one that is more structured than the challenge of deciphering the whole picture, and they enjoy it, laughing as they share an idea. They do take these small problems very seriously, however. When discussing the possible waterway the boat is floating on (another opportunity for some listing), Ben clutches his head in his head and declares with vigour, 'No, that's gotta be in a canal, innit?' (line W16).

Carter (2004) draws on Tannen's research to develop the idea of creative language use. He describes two levels of creative interaction, 'presentational uses of language' (such as puns and metaphors) and 'less overt maybe even subconscious parallels, echoes leading to affective convergence' (2004: 109). The first of these, the 'presentational' puns and metaphors, can be seen to serve a similar purpose to the repetitions described by Tannen above, and also to her suggestion that image creation is a crucial part of a shared construction. They are overt links to the shared experience of the respondent, serving to connect through shared humour or creative images. They lead to both shared understanding and social cohesion, establishing a link between the dialogic readers, which is not just about the speech event itself. They also provide a 'less dense' cognitive space, both for provisional and potential meaning, and work as a buffer for the creation of new ideas. Carter suggests that sometimes, however, these are less overt and this second level of creative interaction is far more subtle. This could perhaps be through voice and tone 'matching' or even through subconsciously employed rhyming, assonance, alliteration or repetition, as highlighted by Tannen. These connections to the previous speaker all carry the same message: 'I am like you, and therefore we will understand each other'. Whether overt or subconscious, the features of the discourse that indicate a shared social goal are fundamental features, as they are a prerequisite to dialogue happening at all. Gina and Sophie (Y6) employ a number of linguistic strategies to 'converge' and their discussion illustrates both of Carter's levels of creative interaction:

01	*Sophie*	That's really actually quite strange.
02	*Gina*	Yeah . . . there's lots of men and they kind of [seem to be] . . .
03	*Sophie*	[Reminds me of] Mary Poppins . . .
04	*Gina*	Hmm, but a male version . . .
05	*Sophie*	. . . of Mary Poppins.

06	*Gina*	And houses . . .
07	*Sophie*	It's <u>like</u> and <u>like</u> they're <u>like</u> just falling down.
08	*Gina*	[mmm] Just falling from the sky . . .
09	*Sophie*	[<u>Like</u>] it's quite . . .
10	*Gina*	It really is raining men . . . (*smiles*)
11	*Sophie*	(*smiles*) yeah.
12	*Gina*	Cos I thought that <u>like</u>, one or two of them had umbrellas, but it's just all loads and loads of others in the background.
13	*Sophie*	Yeah just loads and loads and loads <u>like</u> . . . they're <u>like</u> . . . I wonder what's over those houses, <u>like</u> over them cos there's like men in the distance so . . . I wonder where they're gonna land but you tell that he's gonna land like there or (*points*) that one's gonna land there, and that one's gonna land of top of him (*looks at G – G smiles, both half laugh*).
14	*Gina*	I like that picture.
15	*Sophie*	Yeah . . . Look there are all the little chimneys in the background . . .
16	*Gina*	Or are they people actually falling? (*points and laughs*)
17	*Sophie*	Oh yeah they could be! Look there!
18	*Gina*	Oh yeah, I think they're actually people falling . . .

The first noticeable feature is that they often use the language of agreement, starting turns with 'yeah' even if what follows is a new point (line 15). They also echo each other's language, for example lines 12 and 13, where phrases are repeated. There are also markers they share but that do little to forward the meaning-making. Suggesting that something is 'like' something else or 'kind of' is being indefinite and therefore is open to challenges or alternatives. However, the use of these markers is so common in this discussion that they seem a habit rather than a premeditated functional tool, and it is one that both girls share. It brings them together as they speak with the same pattern and tone, and establishes that they are similar, and therefore share goals.

Wegerif (2005) argues that in addition to the three distinct social modes of thinking put forward by Mercer et al. (1999), there is a fourth 'neglected idea of playful talk' (Wegerif, 2005: 235). He returns to transcripts from his earlier research with Mercer and highlights sequences where the language can still be termed *reasoning* and builds from one response to another, but illustrates a playful or creative approach to the discussion. He argues that 'verbal creativity . . . is an underlying and essential ingredient of the co-construction of meaning in dialogues . . . this includes the case of explicit verbal reasoning' (2005: 235). This sense of the 'playful' reinforces the notion of a dialogic space as it allows a buffer between ideas, buying time between ideas and maintaining the opportunity for inter-thinking. Playful language may not carry deep or extended thinking, but it reinforces the status of the goal as joint enterprise, as speakers share jokes together.

In their discussion about *Golconde*, not only do Sophie and Gina refer to the pop song *It's Raining Men*, they also joke about it, and this joke occurs twice in the discussion. First Gina comments, 'It really is raining men . . . ' (line 10), smiling wryly. That this is a direct reference is made clear by 'really' and Sophie responds by smiling. At this point in the dialogue it is not clear if Sophie actually shares or understands the joke. However, she herself brings the reference up again much later (in line 27 of the dialogue), drawing on the fact that the world of the text must be a fantasy because 'You don't normally see raining men'. She smiles and looks out of the window, commenting, 'No, it's not raining men!' The return to the joke, and the smiles that the children share, can be interpreted as an inter-subjectivity based on this mutual understanding. They are stepping outside the frame of the discussion to smile at their linking of the Magritte picture to a song. They are playing with their shared knowledge to be creative in their language, and using puns and jokes. This inter-subjectivity through humour is also evident in Hannah and Anna's discussion, when Anna suggests that the Lady of Shalott should clean her skirt in a dishwasher:

18	*Anna*	She could put it in a dishwasher couldn't she?
19	*Hannah*	(*Laughs*) . . . dishwasher?!
20	*Anna*	(*Laughs*) No I mean a . . . thingy!

This shared joke offers an opportunity for light relief, even if at the expense of Anna, who takes up the joke and laughs at her own mistake too, realizing that she meant 'washing machine' but is unable to remember the word. This playful approach keeps a light social tone which is epitomized by the pun on 'cat fish' in the discussion that Harry and Ben have about the Waterhouse picture:

W32	Ben	Well they might be like goldfish, like.
W33	Harry	They might be other kinds of fish. They might be haddock.
W34	Ben	Mmm
W35	Harry	Or it might be . . . mmm any other of fish? Might be skate or it might be a cat . . . cat fish . . . ?
W36	Ben	You mean cat fish?
W37	Harry	Yeah . . . Or it might be a cat that's dived in to catch the fish there and [then it kinds like] . . .
W38	Ben	That's the fish . . . and this kind of silvery black bit is the cat.
W39	Harry	Yeah and it's trying to catch it and this lady's gone out to catch the cat and then so she can catch the fish.

The children seem to move easily and playfully between ideas here, both reasoning (from Ben) and building an image to explain their thinking. This verbal creativity allows the children to divergently and creatively co-construct a meaning. However, it could be argued that their success in maintaining social harmony is more subtly achieved than at first assumed. It is Harry who is continuing a list of possible fish that might be in the water. Ben's suggestion that there might be goldfish (line W32) is not just accepted by Harry, who rather than acknowledging the suggestion mentions other types of fish. If Harry's utterances are considered in isolation, it could be argued that he is paying very little attention to Ben's suggestions. Even when Ben asks for clarification, 'You mean cat fish?' (line W36), he replies positively, but almost as if Ben's question is a validation of his own idea which he then develops into his own narrative. When he responds to Ben's attempt to locate the possible cat and fish in the picture, again his response, 'yeah', leads into the extension of his own narrative. It can be argued that he is using agreement to appease the other speaker by creating a façade of social cohesion, while pursuing an individual line of thinking. Of course, Ben does not react to this, and seems happy to continue with Harry's creation, buying into it by adding his own embellishments and justifications (as he did with the helicopter story earlier). The relationship between the two children is surely an influence here, with Harry taking the lead role (remembering that all of the questions about the text are exclusively his) and putting Ben in the position of respondent to ideas rather than generator of them. Ben does, however, make the most of this role, offer interesting justifications for Harry's ideas and seeming to be happily involved in doing so, which is indicated by the intensity of his gesturing and tone in the video vignette.

Agreeing and disagreeing

The suggestion that using the language of agreement might actually serve more subtle purposes than simply agreeing leads to the final theme within the analysis of the social dimension of the children's talk. A dimension of social harmony can be seen as a prerequisite of co-constructive talk, as a shared goal of meaning-making necessitates joint understandings and negotiation. The crucial factor is the balance of harmony and positive critical or dialogic thinking (used as a term to denote the taking of an alternative position). For the dialogic readers, this can be illustrated by cases where there is a disharmony as well as in cases where the children quite skilfully negotiate a joint meaning.

In an example of the former, Bella and Georgia (Y1) are not concerned with seeking or negotiating agreement; they follow their own lines of thinking and represent the only vignette where disagreement is open and transparent. Their disagreements take different forms, both overtly and more subtly when they each ignore the other's ideas. As only excerpts have been included so far, below is included the whole of the transcript from their discussion as they talk together to make meaning from the Klee painting, *They're Biting* (1920).

01	*Bella*	Well . . .
02	*Georgia*	We've got a man and it . . . it . . .
03	*Bella*	Well, there's a woman and it looks like that's curly hair and she's facing that way! (*pointing*)
04	*Georgia*	Yeah, anyway, and it looks like that man is actually putting that in the water.
05	*Bella*	There's a hook.
06	*Georgia*	Yeah, there's a hook and that fish is actually coming through on top of it and it's a very old-fashioned drawing because um these

are old sorts of ways to draw fishes. Isn't it? And it's got a very old . . . (*unclear as Bella interrupts*)

07	Bella	Which fish . . . which part of the picture do you think is really neat?
08	Georgia	Neat? I think all of it! It's very neat!
09	Bella	Well, it looks a bit weird but the thing you can see clearly that's neat is that that and that. (*pointing*)
10	Bella	Yeah and like why is it like an invisible thing?
11	Georgia	And why is that question mark there . . . ? (*pointing*)
12	Bella	It's not a question mark and don't touch!
13	Georgia	Well then it's a clue mark. It's a clue mark, whatever mark but it looks real. It looks so that fish is trying to, um, solve a clue. Isn't it? Isn't it?
14	Bella	Well that sign really means like, doesn't it, hooray! It means like you have to say it in a 'hooray' voice. Whatever word you're saying you need to make it sound like you're actually saying it. (*pause*) Georgia! Get on with it! Well my question is, why's that on it?
15	Georgia	What? That?
16	Bella	That.
17	Georgia	I . . . that's what I was thinking. Why is that there? Yeah and why? And I don't know why they put old fashioned . . . I don't know why what that thing is there. It looks quite old really.
18	Bella	That?
19	Georgia	Yeah, that.
20	Bella	That little line?
21	Georgia	Yeah
22	Bella	Well that's . . .
23	Georgia	(interrupts) that's actually a person!

The disharmony between these speakers is established from the outset with Georgia interrupting Bella's opening statement and claiming the floor, then by Bella restating her opening comment, and following with a suggestion opposite to the previous point, still interested in gender (as with some of the other vignettes); they both decide their individual viewpoint and ignore the other suggestion.

A similar disagreement happens again, later in the discussion, when they discuss what Georgia interprets as a question mark, but this time Bella is quite forthright in telling Georgia that 'It's not a question mark and don't touch!' (line 12). Georgia's response is to rename the 'question mark' as a 'clue mark' (line 13) – still sticking to her initial interpretation, but she does so with an affirming, 'Well then it's a clue mark'. This is interesting, as up to that point in the discussion, 'Well' has been Bella's initiating linguistic marker. Even though the children are talking at odds with each other, they are still picking up the pattern of each other's language. While continuing to disagree, Georgia seeks validation for her ideas by asking 'isn't it?' twice. However, Bella uses the same pattern of language to disagree as she used right at the beginning, starting her turn with a decisive 'Well' then contradicting Georgia's idea (line 14). She also openly reprimands Georgia for not behaving appropriately and then uses her explanation about the 'sign' to prove that Georgia is wrong, rather than as a possible alternative.

This example can be defined as disputational talk (Mercer, 2000) discussed in Chapter 3, as it is not geared towards the joint completion of the task, and sets the dialogue at risk of breaking down. There is not a harmony within this vignette and while the children do respond to each other, there is not an overall collegiality in their discussion. The impact of this is that the success of the task is affected negatively. They are not successfully co-constructing meaning, rather each coming to their own solutions, and there is no space of possibility afforded by this talk as each child is only fixed on completing the task independently of the other. In the other vignettes, even when one child is more dominant (for example, Harry), the other 'buys into' the story and helps to embellish it. Bella and Georgia do not construct any narrative to extend the text, or really very clearly identify what they see in the picture.

The discussion between Tilly and Kate offers a direct contrast to this. As discussed in the previous chapter, it can be seen that these two children are so fixed on the task of joint construction that they do not challenge each other at all, with Kate merely agreeing with Tilly. While this does not present a lack of harmony, it does mean that the children are not using the social dimension of their talk as a tool to invite a co-constructive dialogue. Rather, they use language to give an appearance of deep thinking, and end up with a superficiality in what they are saying. A combination of being too aware of the task, potentially pleasing the teacher (researcher) and a need to get on with each other means that they are unable to engage with any depth.

However, the skilled negotiation of discussion can enhance the potential for creative co-constructive talk. This can be illustrated by Sophie and Gina, who clearly aim for a social harmony and frequently 'agree' with each other, creatively using their language to imitate patterns of speech (discussed above), but this does not mean that they just accept each other's ideas:

15   *Sophie*   Yeah . . . Look there are all the little chimneys in the background . . .
16   *Gina*   Or are they people actually falling? (*points and laughs*)
17   *Sophie*   Oh yeah they could be! Look there!
18   *Gina*   Oh yeah, I think they're actually people falling . . .

In this excerpt, Gina is disagreeing with the suggestion that the figures in the Magritte picture *Golconde* are chimneys, but she does it skilfully. By keeping a light tone, and suggesting an alternative, she is able to correct Sophie. By challenging each other in this way, the children do not compromise the social cohesion of the event and are then able to offer alternatives. In this case the alternative is accepted by Sophie with no loss of social face, and Gina can be more definite in her response, changing from a suggestion and provisional understanding to a firmer statement: the figures are 'actually' people not chimneys. This is an interesting alternative approach to Bella and Georgia's, and demonstrates how the dialogue can continue to operate as co-constructive talk, with both children offering ideas and not proving the other wrong. It could be argued that as older children Sophie and Gina are better able to handle disagreement more sensitively than their Y1 counterparts. However, they are from the same class as Tilly and Kate who manage the discussion poorly, highlighting the many different factors that contribute to a social cohesion. Perhaps they are best friends, or not close friends, or friends who have just argued, or made up? The social intricacies of children's friendships are part of the sociocultural context that affects the way that children learn together – and need handling with sensitivity.

The social negotiation through the dialogic reading event requires more than just the agreement or challenge of ideas. Sometimes the children agree with each other as an initial response, to enable them to then follow up with an alternative or extended idea. In the vignette of Alex and Sam (Y6), this occurs as a complete contradiction in meaning when the children discuss how the boy Shane found the cat in *Way Home*:

11   *Alex*   How did he get that cat in the first place? He like . . .
12   *Sam*   Look if you go back to the beginning (*flicks pages*) it doesn't tell you how he got it does it?
13   *Alex*   Yeah . . . Well it does tell you how he got it
14   *Sam*   (unclear . . . *reading*) . . . alright . . .
15   *Alex*   I was a bit surprised the cat went into there, so quickly, without being really scared.
16   *Sam*   Yeah I know, you walk up to a cat and it just legs it.
17   *Alex*   Yeah, and he just walked up to it and it went straight into his jacket.

Neither child is very clear initially, and line 13 shows Alex to completely contradict himself, initially agreeing and then disagreeing with Sam, though the question about the cat originated with him. The social harmony between the boys suggests that the lack of clarity in these turns does not set the dialogue at risk of breaking down through lack of understanding, nor does it simply indicate a limited cumulative dialogue. After this initial confusion, the children continue to discuss their reactions to that part of the story, empathizing with the main character and returning to previous themes to extend them (full transcript in Chapter 4). They use several agreeing statements and connectives to continue the dialogic chains of thinking.

Agreeing, appearing to agree or disagreeing can be subtle and sophisticated processes with sometimes contradictory consequences. Cumulative talk can serve a useful social underpinning, allowing a more exploratory discussion to emerge, but equally it can limit creative response. Children working completely at odds with each other like Bella and Georgia will clearly find it much harder to develop an inter-subjectivity.

Chapter summary

The meaning made between the dialogic readers in this study includes an interwoven social dimension geared towards cohesion and harmony which enables provisional meaning-making. This is not merely cumulative talk, but underpins the effective co-construction of meaning, as without a basic commitment to a joint endeavour, the talk quickly breaks down, or the potential afforded by exploration and creative thinking is not fulfilled. In these cases the children are less inclined to offer suggestions or explanations, instead defaulting to a mode of statements and justifications that they are 'right' and their partners are 'wrong'. In other vignettes the children find common references to build an inter-subjectivity (Rogoff, 1990: 71), and an important part of this is shared humour. Harry and Ben play on the words 'cat' and 'cat fish' and together build explanatory narratives to make meaning from the text; Sophie and Gina laugh at the cultural reference to *It's Raining Men* and Hannah and Anna giggle about Anna's confusion between a dishwasher and a washing machine. They also show that they value the comments of the other child by extending their ideas, or listing similar connections: Tilly and Kate list the pictures that they like; Alex and Sam list all the names that the cat is given. In fact, even Liam and James conclude their discussion with a 'happily ever after' statement as they both recognize that as the end of a story, so there is nothing else to say. These exchanges are all indicators of a social dimension that the children are aware needs managing. What may appear to be agreement without criticism is not just an indicator of non-challenging, socially orientated, cumulative talk, but a key factor in enabling a creative, problem-finding and divergent co-construction. In the model of co-constructive talk, the underpinning social dimension serves as more than merely a context for the dialogue; it is also a dynamic tool to open and maintain a space for dialogic reading.

Note

1 Another pair of children in the same class of Y6 children, Max and Tom, reflected on their discussion and how different it might have been had it happened away from the classroom. They described how if they had been talking about a visual text at home (in their case, an animated film) without the element of it being a 'task', they would probably not have pursued the conversation for as long as they did before turning to a new subject. As two very frank Y6 children, they were quite open in reflecting that they were not sure there was any value in discussing the film for as long as they did.

8

FROM RESEARCH INTO PRACTICE

This final chapter offers the opportunity to make sense of the research in terms of the most important implication of all: what it might, could or should mean for primary classroom practice. The intentions of the chapter therefore are to draw together the discussion from the previous chapters and build an analytical framework for what being a dialogic reader might be like, and from this position, how effective dialogic reading can be encouraged. Rather than talking about the characteristics of such a reader, I prefer the term 'disposition' as it implies more of a 'stance', a position that leans on the original work of Rosenblatt (1978) who talked of reading 'stances', though hers were related more to purposes for reading (whether to gather information or take pleasure from reading) than an approach taken. Being disposed to act is more than being able to act; it suggests agency and choice. Additionally, the term 'disposition' has been used in the work of Deakin Crick et al. (2004) and Claxton (2007) who describe the dispositions of successful learners who are able to recognize themselves as such and draw on different resources to be so.

It is not enough just to describe this, however, as a responsibility of educational research is to inform improved practice. So after identifying key dispositions for being an effective dialogic reader, the chapter will move on to consider practical applications for the classroom, and then beyond this, implications for progression through primary schooling. The children in this study were drawn from the start and end of primary education, but did their conversations truly show a progression in their co-constructive talk, other than reflecting an increased cultural awareness?

An analytical framework for describing dialogic readers

So what are the dispositions of an effective dialogic reader? The examples from the previous chapters hint at some of the features of a successful dialogic engagement with a text, 'successful' being determined by the children's ability to think together productively and creatively, justifying their reasoning and not being bound by a need to find the 'right' answer. Summarizing from the previous chapters then, dialogic readers can be seen to be:

- critical and creative: questioning, enquiring and challenging
- responsive: flexible and able to build on the ideas of others
- collaborative: able to manage a discussion to best effect and negotiate meanings
- reflective: aware of their own thinking and their task progress within a context.

Of course, the children in the study display these dispositions to a mixed degree. There are flashes of deep, collaborative engagement throughout the vignettes, and even those in which the discussion is less successful, an analysis of what is going wrong helps to draw out what might have made it more positive. Viewing the dispositions as a means of effectively engaging in text allows for some specific observations. Therefore, as the starting point for the study has been the importance of language as an indicator of thinking and collaboration, each of these dispositions is now explored, focusing on how they are indicated through talk in a dialogic reading context.

Being critical and creative: questioning, enquiring and challenging

The starting point for engagement with text in whatever mode it might be presented (visual, moving image, written) is the desire to find out about it, to unlock meanings that might be intended by the creator or to make sense of it in one's own way, prioritizing features with which connections can be made. Texts do not present their meanings to readers; rather, meaning is made in the space between text and reader, and it is an active choice on the part of the reader to start to fill the gaps of meaning (Iser, 1978). They do this by wanting to find out or enquire, and by hypothesizing about what might be. It is the thinking of the hypothesis, the 'what if', that can be seen as dispositional. It implies that what is presented is not enough; that answers might lie beyond the literal, and that horizons can be broadened. Claxton et al. (2006: 58) identify this dispositional element in their writing when they suggest that 'creativity relies not just on the *ability* to think, attend or reflect in certain ways, but on the *inclination* to do so, and to take *pleasure* in doing so' [their emphasis]. To take this further, enquiry is dependent on a disposition to think creatively, or rather, to be *curious*. Notions of curiosity are recognized by Craft, who in summarizing the defining characteristics present in the 'successful possibility thinker' suggests that 'they involve background attitudes of curiosity and sustained openness to integrating thinking with experience, and include the tendency to display intrinsic motivation to explore and create' (2000: 17). This is also reflected in the research work around the Effective Lifelong Learning Inventory (ELLI) where researchers identify a key dimension of effective lifelong learning to be a disposition of 'critical curiosity' (Deakin Crick et al., 2004: 255) whereby a desire to find things out is manifested.

Dialogic readers who approach texts with such a critical curiosity search for meanings and connections. In the vignettes, this thinking is indicated by continual comments: 'I wonder', 'maybe', 'could be', 'perhaps'. These phrases are not always used to form questions, but they open up the thinking into 'possibility'. In the vignettes they are coded as SP-Suggests or Poses or QT-Questions Text. They allow the readers to move beyond the frame of the text and to challenge it, rather than just accepting what is given. In linear, written narratives, these hypotheses are tested and refined as the action unfolds; in more spatial or ambiguous texts, the testing of the hypotheses is reliant on more critical thinking – does this possibility make sense? In Harry and Ben's discussion of Magritte's painting, they use the language of critical curiosity to create the story of helicopters. Anna and Hannah similarly justify their hypothesis that the Lady of Shalott has a dirty skirt. Being curious is not enough though; the readers must also critically challenge the meanings they make to ensure that they are 'reasonable' (Ennis, 1987). They use 'I think' and 'because' to rationalize their suggestions or 'isn't it?' to seek affirmation for their views. In the vignettes, the code RE-Rationalizes or Explains denotes this critical move towards justification.

Being responsive: flexible and able to build on the ideas of others

Dialogic readers respond to the text and to each other. The affordance of the dialogic engagement that they have with each other is the possibility of building on an idea together, responding to suggestions and building a chain of thinking. This is at the heart of 'exploratory talk' and inter-thinking (Mercer, 2000, 2004; Mercer and Littleton, 2007; Littleton and Mercer, 2013). The degree to which the children in the vignettes are able to successfully build on each other's thinking varies, reflecting that they had received little instruction or practice in building ideas in this way. However, there are moments when this happens in each vignette (perhaps Bella and Georgia notwithstanding) and typically, these moments are indicated by longer dialogic chains of thinking. So, for Harry and Ben their longest chain involves fourteen turns (see Chapter 3) and reflects the joint construction of their helicopter story. However, it would be misleading to suggest that sustained thinking only happens in directly linked turns. The case of Alex and Sam sees that they are able to concurrently and recurrently discuss two themes across their dialogue (see Chapter 4) as these chains are more fluid. The key indicators of this chaining, then, are not specific linguistic markers, but repeated words and phrases that signpost a return to an earlier theme, in addition to the use of connectives to link ideas from one turn to the next.

Also worth noting are the cases where the children appear to be engaged in a dialogue, yet really they are not building on each other's ideas at all. Rather, these cases show that the children are involved in their own line of thinking (possibly dialogical) as even though they use common connectives to link with the previous speaker, they are really only pursuing their own thinking. Bella and Georgia show this approach, but even for Harry and Ben who appeared to generate a more exploratory dialogue, it could be argued that Harry is the driver of the ideas, with Ben merely adding detail. While the indicators of exploratory talk, for example 'I think . . . because', might be apparent, the dialogue itself might include little genuine inter-thinking. Similarly, in the case of Liam and James the repetition of 'because' gives the impression of connected thought, yet is being used by the boys to gain, or hold, the floor. These cases are a clear reminder that placing too much emphasis on the use of particular words and phrases might be misleading; the significance is in how the language is used, rather than which words are used.

Being collaborative: able to manage a discussion to the best effect and negotiate meanings

Of course, as seen in Chapter 7, being able to engage in discussion is about more than the content of building ideas. Even the youngest children in this research demonstrate that they are quite sophisticated in the management of their discussions and are able to maintain a social harmony that allows ideas to be shared. The extent to which this building of harmony is intuitive is unclear, with the children picking out the patterns in language and repeating them without realizing, but the results are the same. Where the children mirror each other's language and build on patterns, they achieve an affective convergence (Carter, 2004). The vignettes show how the children use connectives not just to build on ideas as suggested above but also to further the joint endeavour of dialogic reading. In the vignettes, the codes AS-Agrees or Supports and EC-Extends or Continues illustrate parts in their discussion where the dialogic space is maintained and allows room for possibilities. In addition to these links in the syntagmatic dimension of talk (Wells, 1981), the use of clear linguistic markers to denote provisionality, or a hypothetical modality, has the impact of allowing not only for the suggestion of ideas as discussed above but also the negotiation of meaning, with 'Here's an idea, I'm not sure about it, what do you think?' being implied by the use of 'mighten it?', 'isn't it', 'perhaps' and 'maybe'.

Less dependent on specific markers but nevertheless important in the continuation of a shared dialogue are the repetitions that the children make. Again, these enable the building of ideas, but also serve the purpose of establishing connections between speakers and patterns of language that mean the speakers use similar patterns of speech, either through adopting the same phrases – 'like' in the case of Sophie and Gina – or by falling into a pattern of questioning and response. 'I wonder why?' asks Anna repeatedly, to which Hannah replies, 'Maybe . . . ' and 'It's probably . . . '. Compare this pattern to James' and Liam's use of 'I know why' and the social value is the same; the repetitions support a joint approach. However, the subtle difference between 'wondering' and 'knowing' means that the children develop very different ideas, with Liam and James tied more tightly to the events of the text and Anna and Hannah moving beyond the frame of what they see to create new stories.

In addition to the repetition of words and phrases to establish a social harmony, the children make jokes and puns and relate to each other through playfulness in their language (Wegerif, 2005). Examples of these are cultural references (Sophie and Gina), playing with lists (Harry and Ben) or laughing at each other (Anna and Hannah), but they all have the same effect: 'We can laugh together, we are similar'.

Being reflective: aware of their own thinking and their task progress within a context

In Flavell's 1979 article exploring metacognition, he proposes a model that highlights four classes of metacognitive ability: metacognitive knowledge; experience; tasks and goals; and activities and strategies. He argues that the development of these four classes has significant potential for lifelong learning, supporting children and adults to make 'wise and thoughtful life decisions' (1979: 910). The children in this book also demonstrate through their language that they are aware of their own thinking and the progression of the dialogic reading task, and that they understand the context in which it is happening. This allows them to manage their interaction successfully and fulfil the task goals to make meaning from the texts together. However, the metacognitive element of their thinking can be seen to be rather ad hoc. Where there is a misbalance of priority – that is, thinking too much about the task and goals and not about the quality of their thinking in its own right – the meanings the children make are limited (Bella and Georgia) or superficial (Tilly and Kate).

Reflection on the process of their own thinking occurs *in-process* or *on-process*, and there are language indicators that reflect this in the vignettes. As Alex and Sam, who are engaged in a linear narrative text (the picturebook *Way Home*), start to reflect back on the contents of the story, they are also able, in parallel, to comment on how their thinking has developed throughout, to reflect *on-process*. So, 'I thought that . . . ' and 'I was surprised when . . . ' become useful frames from which to hang their thinking. Similarly, but *in-process*, Harry and Ben also reflect on their thinking in parallel to their discussion. There are less specific linguistic markers here, but they are able to judge the value of their thinking as it is happening, almost as an aside to the camera; 'That's a question, isn't it?' remarks Harry. This raises an interesting question. Does the presence of the camera act as a metacognitive reminder to the children, so that they listen to their thoughts with the critical ear that Nickerson et al. (1985) highlight in their work? If so, then it is worth considering how else children might be prompted to reflect *in-action* and to notice more explicitly their thought processes.

The children's awareness of the task they are involved in and the situational context in which it is happening is indicated by the language they use to mark the start and end of their discussion, for example 'Right, what do you think it is first' (Harry) and 'Finished?' (James). Bella's comment to 'Get on with it?!' also indicates a desire to complete the task. These comments show more than just an awareness of the task; they also show a management of it, illustrating that the children can relate their activity to its goals with a sense of how best they might be achieved. They are able to mark the beginning and end of the discussion quite specifically, recognizing that it is an activity to be completed within the context of normal school learning. Where the fulfilment of the task becomes more important than the content of it, the discussion is awkward and stilted. Equally, an over-awareness of the situational context and its embodied values and expectations leads to a shift in focus, and superficial engagement as seen in the vignette of Tilly and Kate's conversation.

What might happen in the classroom?

If these observations of language illustrate a framework for dialogic reading, then our attention now turns to the classroom and the environment that might promote such talk. Much of Mercer's work with different colleagues over the last twenty years (Mercer, 1995, 1996; Mercer et al., 1999; Mercer, 2000, 2004; Mercer and Littleton, 2007; Littleton and Mercer, 2013) has identified the importance of not only building talk opportunities for children to think together, but also supporting them in understanding 'ground rules' for talk, so that they can manage their discussions to best effect (Thinking Together, 2014). The authors find that without explicit teaching, much of what children say is not truly exploratory and is often cumulative or disputational. The close analysis of children's talk in this study shows that even without explicit instruction, children can work dialogically together and manage their discussions with some sophistication. However, rather than assuming that children can and do naturally engage in this way, we can use these illustrations as indicators of the types of language and interactions that the children should encounter as part of a rich reading curriculum, and the types of activities that might promote these.

If we want to hear children using particular language, then it is important that as teachers we model it. I remember with amusement overhearing children from my then Y6 class talking in the playground and using phrases and words I knew were typical of me. It reminded me that I needed to be thoughtful in my language use with them, particularly when playing with words and making puns. In the vignettes there are a couple of instances where adult voices are mimicked. There is a strong sense in the vignette of Tilly and Kate that they are role-playing with a particular style of interaction, engaging seriously and having a deep discussion, trying out the mode. In other examples, both Bella and Harry take on a teacherly stance in their approach to the task. This central learning approach of imitation can be used to good effect.

The analytic framework above gives some key language indicators that teachers can use to demonstrate to children how they engage with texts and other readers themselves, but this can be extended. A recent Film Talk research project working alongside teachers and using short animated film to promote comprehension strategies (Maine and Shields, 2015) concentrated on using key language in reciprocal small group teaching activities. Strategies for comprehension were matched with talk prompts to support the children to frame their ideas. The role of the teacher was to model these, so that instead of questioning the children by, for example, asking, 'What does it remind you of?', they used the language themselves, so modelled 'That reminds me of . . . '. In this way, the children were clear about what the language of comprehension sounded like, and were able to use it, even when the teacher took a step back and encouraged the children to develop the discussion by themselves (following the work of Palincsar and Brown, 1984). Table 8.1 links the different comprehension strategies that were identified in Chapter 5 to key language that could be promoted to encourage that thinking, building on the words

TABLE 8.1 The language of dialogic engagement with text

Comprehension strategy	Language to model and encourage (talk prompts)
Determining importance and making connections to existing knowledge	The most important parts were . . . First, then, next . . . The main point was . . . It reminds me of . . . It made me think about . . . If . . . then . . . I noticed that . . .
Asking questions and making predictions	I wonder if . . . Why? What is it all about? Maybe . . . Possibly . . . Perhaps . . . I think . . . because . . . It means . . . . I think what will happen is . . . because
Empathizing with characters and entering the text-world	If it was me I would have . . . I think he/she felt . . . It's scary/exciting/funny when . . . It made me feel . . . I could imagine . . . I understand how he/she feels I would too . . .
Self-monitoring and metacognition	It confused me when . . . I'm not sure why . . . I was surprised when . . . I thought that . . . I liked it when . . . I didn't like . . .

and phrases that the children are already using. Specific language indicators are not always appropriate, and therefore there are no specific talk prompts to support children to create narratives and images to extend the text-world; rather, these are created by the same hypothetical language used to prompt questioning and prediction. Included in the table are also talk prompts for encouraging self-monitoring and metacognition, to support children's awareness of their thought processes and possible misconceptions.

The importance of the teacher modelling uncertainties and doubts moves beyond simply demonstrating language into setting up an exploratory ethos in the classroom, where children feel comfortable analyzing their misunderstandings and sharing their confusions. Within a typical UK primary classroom, reading opportunities happen on three levels: within the whole class, in small groups and independently. The first two particularly offer a chance for children to engage with other readers, while in the third independent activity, their dialogic engagement is with the text itself, but with the potential of a dialogical thinking voice (Paul, 1987). Sharing texts with the whole class offers the perfect opportunity for teachers to model what it is to be a dialogic reader, to show how they themselves engage with texts and with the views of the children in the class. This approach sits neatly within the dialogic teaching framework espoused by Alexander (2008) and the Cambridge Primary Review (Alexander, 2010) as it invites genuine discussion and exploration by teacher and children in an environment where children are encouraged to listen to each other, challenge each other and engage with dialogue that is not dominated by the teacher. Talk prompts such as those suggested in Table 3 can provide a useful scaffold for this dialogue to encourage children to entangle themselves with the text, alongside the teacher.

However, the small group reading setting has the most potential for the close teaching and modelling of dialogic engagement. 'Guided reading' was promoted in England as an essential pedagogical tool for supporting readers of similar abilities, with effective guided reading very carefully geared towards supporting children's responses to text (Bearne, 2008). The small group provides an opportunity for a reciprocal teaching approach and for children to develop genuine responses to text. In a study exploring how children responded to classic children's fiction (Maine and Waller, 2011), small groups of children were given talk prompts to support them to talk together based on Chambers' 'Tell Me' approach (1993). They were then able to conduct their discussion as an independent reading group while the teacher worked with another more 'guided' reading group. They recorded their discussion for the teacher to listen to and assess their understanding and ability to talk together to make meaning. In an already inundated educational context, it is important that ideas for developing improved practice can be implemented within existing structures, and the group reading environment in primary schools is perfect for this.

The approach of this book has been to embrace written, visual and moving image media as equal in their affordance for promoting reading comprehension. There is a further suggestion (Maine and Shields, 2015) that using visual texts as a resource to specifically focus on comprehension instruction is highly beneficial as the cognitive strain of decoding words is removed, allowing a greater engagement with a pursuit of meaning beyond the literal. A mixture of spatial and linear texts also supports children's understanding of the texts that surround them in the 21st century. There is an implication for teachers, however, who need to know how to access quality multi-modal texts and to build up a bank of such resources, in addition to thinking through the affordance of each different text, particularly those with alternative reading pathways. Moving image media is of particular importance here, as it is a mode with which children have an existing familiarity. Bazalgette (2010) argues that their experiences of film outside school mean they are able to comprehend sophisticated narrative structures in these modes beyond their abilities with written text modes. Although the films they experience most frequently are likely to be longer feature-length films, the affordance of short narratives is significant. Sometimes only two or three minutes in length, the films offer text as a *whole* yet often include ambiguities in meaning and many gaps for readers to fill. In the Film Talk project, the children were motivated by the use of wordless animations. With no language in the texts at all, the concentration could rest entirely with the language of co-construction. The children were able to draw on their existing film knowledge to make sense of what they were seeing, testing out the talk prompt language, which the teachers then used in discussion about other verbal texts.

There remains a further challenge. What progression can we expect children to make throughout primary school in order that they become sophisticated dialogic readers? The children in this study were selected from Y1 and Y6. These year groups mark the span of the primary age phase in the UK, and while the data set was small, it would be reasonable to expect that older children could engage with each other and with the texts with greater sophistication. But did they? Being careful not to generalize about all children, when the seven case studies celebrated a 'particulization' (Stake, 1995), the data indicate that the most creative responses are from Harry, Ben, Anna and Hannah, all Y1 children. Because they are confident and able to manage the task and each other successfully, they are creative in their approach, and able to build on each other's ideas. In Y6, Sophie and Gina are more limited in their responses, without expanding beyond the literal scene, even though the visual text that they encounter, *Golconde*, generates creative narratives from the Y1 children. However, with more linear texts, Liam and James (Y1) struggle to do more than re-tell the story, where Alex and Sam (Y6) are able to generate a more critical discussion about *Way Home* in which they extend the story-world to make sense of it, inferring meaning and reading between the lines.

Where the social management of the discussion is successful, children are able to respond to each other, agreeing or disagreeing through a variety of strategies. Yet there is little to separate the Y1 and Y6 approaches to this, other than to note that as disputational as Bella and Georgia's (Y1) talk is, Sophie and Gina in Y6 seem to cumulatively prioritize the social dimension of their talk to the detriment of a more creative response. Tilly and Kate (Y6), too, are overly aware of the task and produce a limited cumulative response. However, Alex and Sam are able to challenge each other over misconceptions and create joint meanings in a more exploratory fashion. In the project extension when I revisited Harry and Ben in Y6, I found, perhaps not surprisingly, that they were far more conscious of the task and agreeing with each other.

So what might we expect from children at the end of primary school? In their dialogic engagement with text, we might want them to be as creative as they were in Y1, perhaps with a little more criticality in the reasoning of their thinking and problem-solving, without losing the playfulness of their talk, but testing themselves to pursue meaning and challenge their own interpretations. In terms of their dialogic engagement with each other, six years of working in collaborative environments where teachers promote children's engagement with each other and expect them to be able to challenge each other without a risk to their social harmony should surely enable them to work in a more exploratory way. If these dispositions are supported by an approach where children are routinely expected to reflect on their thinking, and to recognize their successes and task management, then a solid foundation of lifelong learning should be set.

Dialogic reading: a theory for 21st-century literacy

Using the term 'dialogic' situates this study and the resulting theoretical framework firmly within more recent thinking about education, and certainly aligns it with a dialogic teaching approach (Alexander, 2008; Lyle, 2008; Alexander, 2010). Here, though, rather than the dialogic space being between pedagogy/pedagogue and learner, the space is between readers together and between text and reader (Maine, 2013). The idea of a transaction between reader and text is not new (Rosenblatt, 1978), but that this might be a dialogical engagement adds to a sociocultural understanding that accepts the space between texts and readers as a fluid and flexible place: a *dialogic space of possibility*. Raising questions and linking connections enables the creation of narratives and images to make meaning. While the study is concerned primarily with visual texts (images, moving images and picturebooks), a choice that meant that non-fluent readers of written text would not be limited by the challenge of decoding words, the discussions that ensue and the language that is highlighted in them transcend text mode. Clearly, spatial and linear texts offer different reading pathways (Kress and van Leeuwen, 1996; Kress, 2003) and this might have an impact on the types of discussion that follow, but the principles of a dialogic reading approach still apply. Arguably, if, as Kress suggests, reading can be defined as 'making sense of the world around me' (2003: 140), then this dialogic framework has much wider applications for young children to be critical, creative, responsive, collaborative and reflective.

REFERENCES

Alexander, R.J. (2003) *Talk for learning: the first year*, Northallerton: North Yorkshire County Council.
—— (2008) *Towards dialogic teaching: rethinking classroom talk*, 4th edn, Cambridge: Dialogos.
Alexander, R.J. (ed.) (2010) *Children, their world, their education: final report and recommendations of the Cambridge Primary Review*, Abingdon: Routledge.
Anderson, R.C. and Pearson, P.D. (1984) 'A schema-theoretic view of basic processes in reading comprehension' in D. Pearson (ed.), *The handbook of reading research*, London: Longman.
Anderson, R.C., Nguyen-Jahiel, K., McNurlen, B., Archodidou, A., Kim, S., Reznitskaya, A., Tillmanns, M., Gilbert, L. (2001) 'The snowball phenomenon', *Cognition and Instruction* 19 (1), 1–46.
Arizpe, E. (2013) 'Meaning-making from wordless (or nearly wordless) picturebooks: what educational research expects and what readers have to say', *Cambridge Journal of Education* 43 (2), 163–176.
Arizpe, E. and Styles, M. (2003) *Children reading pictures interpreting visual text*, London: Routledge.
Bakhtin, M.M. (1981) *The dialogic imagination*, trans. C. Emerson and M. Holquist, Austin, TX: University of Texas Press.
Barnes, D. and Todd, F. (1995) *Communication and learning revisited: making meaning through talk*, Portsmouth, NH: Cook Publishing.
Barthes, R. (1977) *Image music text*, London: Fontana.
—— (1981) 'Theory of the text' trans. I. McLeod in R. Young (ed.), *Untying the text: a post structuralist reader*, London: Routledge.
Bassey, M. (1999) *Case study research in educational settings*, Buckingham: Oxford University Press.
Bazalgette, C. (2010) 'Extending children's experience of film' in C. Bazalgette (ed.), *Teaching media in primary schools*, London: Sage.
Bazalgette, C. and Buckingham, D. (2013) 'Literacy, media and multimodality: a critical response', *Literacy* 47 (2), 95–102.

Bearne, E., Clark, C., Johnson, A., Manford, P., Mottram, M. and Wolstencraft, H. (2007) *Reading on screen*, Leicester: UKLA.

Bearne, E. (ed.) (2008) *Guided reading using short texts at KS2*, Leicester: UKLA.

Benton, M. (2004) 'Reader-response criticism' in P. Hunt (ed.), *International companion encyclopedia of children's literature*, London: Routledge.

Bloom, B. (1956) *A taxonomy of educational objectives*, New York: Longman.

Bloome, D. and Greene, J. (1984) 'Directions in the sociolinguistic study of reading' in D. Pearson (ed.), *The handbook of reading research*, London: Longman.

British Educational Research Association (2011) *Ethical guidelines for educational research*. Available from: www.bera.ac.uk/researchers-resources/publications/ethical-guidelines-for-educational-research-2011 (accessed 12 November 2014).

Bruner, J. (1986) *Actual minds, possible worlds*, London: Harvard University Press.

Burnard, P., Craft, A. and Cremin, T. with Duffy, B., Hanson, R., Keene, J., Haynes, L. and Burns, D. (2006) 'Documenting "possibility thinking": a journey of collaborative enquiry', *International Journal of Early Years Education* 14 (3), 243–262.

Carter, R. (2004) *Language and creativity: the art of common talk*, London: Routledge.

Chambers, A. (1993) *Tell me: children, reading and talk*, Stroud: Thimble Press.

Claxton, G. (2007) 'Expanding young people's capacity to learn', *British Journal of Educational Studies* 55 (2), 115–134.

Claxton, G. with Edwards, L. and Scale-Constantinou, V. (2006) 'Cultivating creative mentalities: a framework for education', *Thinking Skills and Creativity* 1 (1), 57–61.

Cohen, L., Manion, L. and Morrison, K. (2011) *Research methods in education*, 7th edn, Abingdon: Routledge.

Corden, R. (2000) *Literacy and learning through talk: strategies for the classroom*, Oxford: Oxford University Press.

Craft, A. (2000) *Creativity across the curriculum: framing and developing practice*, London: Routledge.

Damico, J.S., Campano, G. and Harste, J.C. (2009) 'Transactional theory and critical theory in reading comprehension' in S. Israel and G.G. Duffy (eds), *Handbook of research on reading comprehension*, London: Routledge, 177–188.

Deakin Crick, R., Broadfoot, P. and Claxton, G. (2004) 'Developing an effective lifelong learning inventory: the ELLI project', *Assessment in Education* 11 (3), 247–272.

Dewey, J. (1933) *How we think*, Boston: D.C. Heath and Co.

Dole, J., Duffy, G.G., Roehler, L.R. and Pearson, P.D. (1991) 'Moving from the old to the new: research on reading comprehension instruction', *Review of Educational Research* 61 (2), 239–264.

Dombey, H. (2010) 'Interaction and learning to read: towards a dialogic approach' in D. Wyse, R. Andrews and J. Hoffman (eds), *The Routledge international handbook of English, language and literacy teaching*, London: Routledge.

Donaldson, M. (1978) *Children's minds*, London: Harper Collins.

Duriez, C. (2003) 'Baboon on the moon' in *Starting stories*, London: British Film Institute.

Edwards, A.D. and Westgate, D.P.G. (1987) *Investigating classroom talk*, Lewes: Falmer Press.

Ennis, R.H. (1987) 'A taxonomy of critical thinking dispositions and abilities' in J.B. Baron and R.J. Sternberg (eds), *Teaching thinking skills: theory and practice*, New York: Fireman and Co.

Fairclough, N. (1992) *Discourse and social change*, Oxford: Blackwell.

Fisher, E. (1993) 'Distinctive features of pupil–pupil classroom talk and their relationship to learning: how discursive exploration might be encouraged', *Language and Education* 17 (4), 239–257.

Flavell, J.H. (1979) Metacognition and cognitive monitoring: a new area of cognitive-developmental inquiry, *American Psychologist* 34 (10), 906–911.

Gaarder, J. (1997) *Hello? Is anybody there?* London: Orion Children's Books.

Gavelek, J. and Bresnahan, P. (2009) 'Ways of meaning making: sociocultural perspectives on reading comprehension' in S. Israel and G.G. Duffy (eds), *Handbook of research on reading comprehension*, London: Routledge, 140–176.

Gergen, K. (1999) *An invitation to social construction*, London: Sage.

Glaser, B. and Strauss, A. (1967) *The discovery of grounded theory: strategies for qualitative research*, New York: Aldine de Gruyter.

Goodman, K. (1967) 'Reading: a psycholinguistic guessing game', *Journal of the Reading Specialist* 6 (4), 126–135.

Habermas, J. (1984) *The theory of communicative action volume 1: reason and the rationalisation of society*, trans. T. McCarthy, London: Heinemann.

Halliday, M.A.K. (1993) 'Towards a language based theory of learning', *Linguistics and Education* 5, 93–116.

Hardy, B. (1977) 'Narrative as a primary act of mind' in M. Meek, A. Warlow and G. Barton (eds), *The cool web: the pattern of children's reading*, London: The Bodley Head.

Harre, R. (1990) 'Exploring the human umwelt' in R. Bhaskar (ed.), *Harre and his critics*, Oxford: Blackwell.

Hassett, D.D. (2010) 'New literacies in the elementary classroom: the instructional dynamics of visual texts' in K. Hall, U Goswami, C. Harrison, S. Ellis and J. Soler (eds), *Interdisciplinary perspectives on learning to read: culture, cognition and pedagogy*. London: Routledge.

Hathorn, L. and Rogers, G. (1994) *Way home*, London: Red Fox.

Hudson, L. (1968) *Frames of mind: ability, perception and self-perception in the arts and sciences*, London: Methuen.

Hymes, D. (1972) 'Models of interaction in language and social life' in J.J. Gumperz and D. Hymes (eds), *Directions in sociolinguistics, the ethnography of communication*, London: Basil Blackwell.

—— (1977) *Foundations in sociolinguistics: an ethnographic approach*, London: Tavistock Publ. Ltd.

Iser, W. (1978) *The act of reading: a theory of aesthetic response*, London: Routledge and Kegan Paul.

Keats, J., Gitings, R. and Mee, J. (2002) *Selected letters: John Keats*, 2nd edn, Oxford: Oxford University Press.

Keene, E. and Zimmerman, S. (1997) *Mosaic of thought: teaching comprehension in a reader's workshop*, Portsmouth, NH: Heinemann.

Klee, P. (1920) *They're biting*, watercolour over oil-colour drawing on paper, 31cm × 23.5cm, The Tate Collection, The Tate Gallery, London. Available from: www.tate.org.uk/art/artworks/klee-theyre-biting-n05658 (accessed 18 July 2014).

Kress, G. (2003) *Literacy in the new media age*, London: Routledge.

—— (2010) *Multimodality: a semiotic approach to contemporary communication*, London: Routledge.

Kress, G. and van Leeuwen, T. (1996) *Reading images: the grammar of visual design*, London: Routledge.

Kumpulainen, K. and Wray, D. (2002) *Classroom interaction and social learning*, London: RoutledgeFalmer.

Leo, J. and Mandelker, A. (1994) 'Author's note', *PMLA* 109 (3), 377.

Lewis, M. and Tregenza, J. (2007) 'Beyond simple comprehension', *English 4-11* 30 (Summer), 11–16.

Lipman, M. (2003) *Thinking in education*, Cambridge: Cambridge University Press.

Littleton, K. and Mercer, N. (2013) *Interthinking: putting talk to work*, Abingdon, Routledge.

Lotman, Y.M. (1994) 'The text within the text' trans. J. Leo and A. Mandelker in *PMLA* 109 (3), 377–384.

Lyle, S. (1993) 'An investigation into the ways in which children "talk themselves into meaning"', *Language and Education* 7 (3), 181–197.

—— (2000) 'Narrative understanding: developing a theoretical context for understanding how children make meaning in classroom settings', *Journal of Curriculum Studies* 32 (1), 45–63.

—— (2002) 'Talking to learn: the voices of children aged 9–11, engaged in role-play', *Language and Education* 16 (4), 303–317.

—— (2008) 'Dialogic teaching: discussing theoretical contexts and reviewing evidence from classroom practice', *Language and Education* 22 (3), 222–240.

Mackey, M. (2007) *Literacies across media: playing the text*, 2nd edn, London: Routledge.

Magritte, R. (1953) *Golconde*, oil on canvas, 81cm × 100cm, The Menil Collection, Houston, TX.

Maine, F. (2013) 'How children talk together to make meaning from texts: a dialogic perspective on reading comprehension', *Literacy* 47 (3), 150–156.

—— (2014) '"I wonder if they are going up or down": children's co-constructive talk across the primary years', *Education 3-13: International Journal of Primary, Elementary and Early Years Education* 42 (3) 298–312.

Maine, F. and Shields, R. (2015) 'Developing reading comprehension with moving image narratives', *Cambridge Journal of Education*. DOI: 1080/0305764X.2014.998625

Maine, F. and Waller, A. (2011) 'Swallows and amazons forever: how adults and children engage in reading a classic text', *Children's Literature in Education* 42 (4), 354–371.

Maybin, J. (1994) 'Children's voices: talk, knowledge and identity' in D. Graddol, J. Maybin and B. Stierer (eds), *Researching language and literacy in social context*, Clevedon: Multilingual Matters.

Mercer, N. (1995) *The guided construction of knowledge: talk among teachers and learners*, Clevedon: Multilingual Matters.

—— (1996) 'The quality of talk in children's collaborative activity in the classroom', *Language and Instruction* 6 (4), 359–377.

—— (2000) *Words and minds: how we use language to think together*, London: Routledge.

—— (2004) 'Sociocultural discourse analysis: analysing classroom talk as a social mode of thinking', *Journal of Applied Linguistics* 1 (2), 137–168.

Mercer, N. and Littleton, K. (2007) *Dialogue and the development of children's thinking: a socio-cultural approach*, Abingdon: Routledge.

Mercer, N., Wegerif, R. and Dawes, L. (1999) 'Children's talk and the development of reasoning in the classroom', *British Educational Research Journal* 25 (1), 95–112.

Moseley, D., Baumfield, V., Elliott, J., Gregson, M., Higgins, S., Miller, J. and Newton, D.P. (2005) *Frameworks for thinking: a handbook for teaching and learning*, Cambridge: Cambridge University Press.

National Advisory Committee on Creative and Cultural Education (NACCCE) (1999) *All our futures: creativity, culture and education*, London: Department for Education and Employment.

National Reading Panel (NRP) (2002) *Teaching children to read: an evidence-based assessment of the scientific research literature on reading and its implications for reading instructions, reports of the subgroups.* Available from: www.nichd.nih.gov/publications/pubs/nrp/Documents/report.pdf (accessed 18 July 2014).

Nickerson, R.S. (1999) 'Enhancing creativity' in R.J. Sternberg (ed.), *Handbook of creativity*, Cambridge: Cambridge University Press.

Nickerson, R.S., Perkins, D.N. and Smith, E.E. (1985) *The teaching of thinking*, New Jersey: Lawrence Erlbaum.

Nikolajeva, M. (2014) 'Picturebooks and emotional literacy', *The Reading Teacher* 67 (4) 249–254.

Nystrand, M. with Gamoran, A., Kachur, R. and Prendergast, C. (1997) *Opening dialogue: understanding the dynamics of language and learning in the English classroom*, London: Teachers College Press.

Palincsar, A. (2003) 'Collaborative approaches to comprehension instruction' in A. Sweet and C. Snow (eds), *Rethinking reading comprehension*, London: The Guilford Press.

Palincsar, A. and Brown, A. (1984) 'Reciprocal teaching of comprehension-fostering and comprehension-monitoring activities', *Cognition and Instruction* 1 (2) 117–175.

Pardo, L. (2004) 'What every teacher needs to know about comprehension', *The Reading Teacher* 58 (3), 272–280.

Paul, R.W. (1987) 'Dialogical thinking: critical thought essential to the acquisition of rational knowledge and passions' in J.B. Baron and R.J. Sternberg (eds), *Teaching thinking skills: theory and practice*, New York: Fireman and Co.

Pearson, P.D. (2009) 'The roots of reading comprehension instruction' in G. Duffy and S. Israel (eds), *Handbook of research on reading comprehension*, London: Routledge, 3–31.

Phillips, T. (1985) 'Beyond lip-service: discourse developments after the age of nine' in G. Wells and J. Nicholls (eds), *Language and learning: an interactional perspective*, London: The Falmer Press.

Piaget, J. (1959) *The language and thought of the child*, 3rd edn, London: Routledge.

Pollard, A. with Filer, A. (1996) *The social world of children's learning*, London: Cassell.

Pressley, M. (2000) 'What should comprehension instruction be the instruction of?' in M. Kamil, P. Mosenthal, P.D. Pearson and R. Barr (eds), *Handbook of reading research, Vol. III*, London: Lawrence Erlbaum.

—— (2006) *Reading instruction that works: the case for balanced teaching*, 3rd edn, London: The Guilford Press.

Protherough, R. (1983) *Developing a response to fiction*, Milton Keynes: Open University.

Quellmalz, E.S. (1987) 'Developing reasoning skills' in J.B. Baron and R.J. Sternberg (eds), *Teaching thinking skills: theory and practice*, New York: Fireman and Co.

RAND Reading Study Group (RRSG) (2002) *Reading for understanding: toward an R+D program in reading comprehension*, Santa Monica, CA: RAND. Available from: www.rand.org/content/dam/rand/pubs/monograph_reports/2005/MR1465.pdf (accessed 18 July 2014).

Reznitskaya, A., Kuo, L.J., Clark, A., Miller, B., Jadallah, M., Anderson, R.C. and Nguyen-Jahiel, K. (2009) 'Collaborative reasoning: a dialogic approach to group discussion', *Cambridge Journal of Education* 39 (1), 29–48.

Robinson, K. (2001) *Out of our minds: learning to be creative*, Oxford: Capstone.

Rogoff, B. (1990) *Apprenticeship in thinking: cognitive development in social context*, Oxford: Oxford University Press.

—— (2003) *The cultural nature of human development*, Oxford: Oxford University Press.

Rojas-Drummond, S., Albarran, C. and Littleton, K. (2008) 'Collaboration, creativity and the co-construction or oral and written texts', *Thinking Skills and Creativity* 1 (3), 177–191.

Rojas-Drummond, S., Mazon, N., Fernandez, M. and Wegerif, R. (2006) 'Explicit reasoning, creativity and co-construction in primary school children's collaborative activities', *Thinking Skills and Creativity* 1 (1), 84–94.

Rosenblatt, L. (1978) *The reader, the text, the poem: the transactional theory of the literary work*, Carbondale, IL: Southern Illinois University Press.

Saussure, F. de (1983) *Course in general linguistics*, trans. R. Harris, London: Duckworth.

Schindler, C. (2002) 'Otherwise (Anders Artig)' in *Starting stories*, London: British Film Institute.

Sinclair, J. and Coulthard, R. (1975) *Towards an analysis of discourse: the English used by teachers and pupils*, Oxford: Oxford University Press.

Smith, F. (1985) *Reading*, 2nd edn, Cambridge: Cambridge University Press.

—— (1988) *Understanding reading*, 4th edn, London: Lawrence Erlbaum.

Smith, V. (2010) 'Comprehension as a social act' in K. Hall, U. Goswami, C. Harrison, S. Ellis and J. Soler (eds), *Interdisciplinary perspectives on learning to read: culture, cognition and pedagogy*, London: Routledge.

Snow, C. and Sweet, A. (2003) 'Reading for comprehension' in A. Sweet and C. Snow (eds), *Rethinking reading comprehension*, London: The Guilford Press.

Soter, A., Wilkinson, I., Murphy, K., Rudge, L., Reninger, K. and Edwards, M. (2008) 'What the discourse tells us: talk and indicators of high-level comprehension', *International Journal of Educational Research* 47, 372–391.

Stake, R.E. (1995) *The art of case study research*, London: Sage.

Stenhouse, L. (1988) 'Case study methods' in J.P. Reeves (ed.), *Educational research, methodology, and measurement: an international handbook*, 2nd edn, Oxford: Pergamon.

Swain, C. (2010) '"It looked like one thing but when we went in more depth, it turned out to be completely different": reflections on the discourse of guided reading and its role in fostering critical response to magazines', *Literacy* 44 (3), 131–136.

Tannen, D. (1989) *Talking voices: repetition, dialogue and imagery in conversational discourse*, Cambridge: Cambridge University Press.

Taylor, R. (2012) Messing about with metaphor: multi-modal aspects to children's creative meaning making, *Literacy* 46 (3), 156–166.

Todorov, T. (1982) *Symbolism and interpretation*, trans. C. Porter, New York: Cornell University Press.

University of Cambridge Faculty of Education (2014) Thinking Together Project. Available from: https://thinkingtogether.educ.cam.ac.uk (accessed 18 July 2014).

Vygotsky, L. (1962) *Thought and language*, Massachusetts: MIT Press.

—— (1978) *Mind in society*, London: Harvard University Press.

Ward, T.B., Smith, S.M. and Finke, R.A. (1999) 'Creative cognition' in R.J. Sternberg (ed.), *Handbook of creativity*, Cambridge: Cambridge University Press.

Waterhouse, J. (1888) *The Lady of Shalott*, oil on canvas. 153cm x 200cm, The Tate Collection, The Tate Gallery, London. Available from: www.tate.org.uk/art/artworks/waterhouse-the-lady-of-shalott-n01543 (accessed 18 July 2014).

Wegerif, R. (2005) 'Reason and creativity in classroom dialogues', *Language and Education* 19 (3), 223–237.

—— (2008a) *Dialogic education and technology: expanding the space of learning*, New York: Springer.

—— (2008b) 'Dialogic or dialectic? The significance of ontological assumptions in research on educational dialogue', *British Educational Research Journal* 34 (3), 347–361.

Wells, G. (1981) *Learning through interaction: the study of language development*, Cambridge: Cambridge University Press.

—— (1999) *Dialogic inquiry: towards a socio-cultural practice and theory of education*, Cambridge: Cambridge University Press.

—— (2009) *The meaning makers: learning to talk and talking to learn*, 2nd edn, Bristol: Multilingual Matters.

Wertsch, J. (1991) *Voices of the mind*, Harvard: Harvard University Press.

Wolf, M.K., Crosson, A. and Resnick, L. (2005) 'Classroom talk for rigorous reading comprehension instruction', *Reading Psychology* 26, 27–53.

Wood, D. (1998) *How children think and learn,* 2nd edn, Oxford: Blackwell.

INDEX

Printed in Great Britain
by Amazon